Memoirs

The Extraordinary Story of a Cuban Prodigy

A Novel Based on True Events

From the author of
Waiting on Zapote Street,
winner of the Latino Books Into Movies
Award, Drama TV Series category
and
Brothers: The Pedro Pan Boys
Winner of the International Latino Books
Awards, Best Fiction Novel category

Betty Viamontes

The Pianist:

The Extraordinary Story of a Cuban Prodigy

Published in the United States by

Zapote Street Books, LLC, Tampa, Florida

Book cover by SusanasBooks LLC

This book contains elements of creative nonfiction.

ISBN: 978-1-955848-31-2

Printed in the United States of America

I dedicate this book to—

Lázara Portomeñe, for inspiring me to write this novel, and to her brother, Alfredo—amazing brother, father, and human being.

My mother, for showing me that anything is possible.

My beloved husband and my family, for all their support.

My loyal readers, for reading my books and encouraging me to keep writing.

The members of all the book clubs who so kindly have chosen to read *Waiting on Zapote Street, The Dance of the Rose, Candela's Secrets and Other Havana Stories, Havana: A Son's Journey Home,* and *The Girl from White Creek* for group discussions.

To Facebook groups *All Things Cuban* for providing a space for sharing stories and culture of the Cuban people and *Women Reading Great Books* for creating a forum for authors and readers to meet.

"A story that encompasses a lifetime. It is rich in imagery, and it is sometimes light and funny, despite the seriousness of the backdrop of a Cuba still in chains." Susana Jiménez-Mueller, international podcaster and creator of *The Green Plantain – The Cuban Series Project* and author of *Now I Swim*.

"An amazing story that spans decades. It takes readers on a roller coaster ride of highs and lows and keeps them wanting to know what's around the corner. Then, when the ride seems to end, there's one last surprise waiting." Conchita Hernández Hicks, author of *Leaving Havana.*

Chapter 1

It's Just Me

I stand by the side of the road and anxiously watch the approaching Cuban embassy bus rolling over debris. The skies are blue today, but when we look around us, the place looks like a war zone, with several buildings reduced to rubble. At last, my group and I are getting rescued! I thought it would never happen, that we would die of hunger and thirst in the place that I had considered a paradise only a few days ago. It's incredible how life can change so quickly, making us question everything we know to be true.

I never thought I would feel happy to return to the place so many want to leave. Yet, I dream of being back home. Many of my friends would give their right arm for the opportunity to live elsewhere. Some of my group members thought the same way until a few days ago. But then the unthinkable happened. If I hadn't known better, I would have thought that nature was scheming against us.

But let me not get ahead of myself. This is not where I wanted to start the story. Not that it was *my* idea to tell you about the sequence of events that brought me here. A writer expressed interest in telling my story and convinced me to share it.

It's Just Me

I have no idea why anyone would care about me. It's not as if I've contributed significantly to the world, like inventing windows and doors that can withstand a category-five hurricane. Where were those windows and doors a few days ago when I needed them? My cousin Gustavo, who lives in the United States, invented them a few years ago, and no one has written *his* story. Go figure. I'll never understand humanity.

Soon, I will return to my life, my tiny apartment, two rocking chairs, and the old mattress that punishes my joints every night. I will return to the old coffee maker I only use when visitors come.

I live alone in a second-story apartment in an unpainted building in Centro Habana. The building was erected in the fifties, so it's in much better shape than those I see when I walk on the streets of Old Havana.

My friends tell me I make them laugh, maybe because I don't take life too seriously. Like Celia Cruz said in her song, "*La vida es un carnaval.*" Life is a carnival. That is my motto. When you look at life like I do, things that ordinarily make you want to bang your head against the wall suddenly seem more palatable. And God knows that my life has been replete with such things.

I'm seventy-something (why keep counting after 70). But I don't feel my age because I stay active and eat little. I had a dog who died six months ago. He was my companion and confidant. If you own a pet, you might understand how close we can get to them. I talked to mine about everything. Sometimes, I would ask him, "Can you believe how long I was standing in line at the grocery store?"

He sat there and listened to me as a good friend would. So, when he died, only a handful of meters away from me, on top of a doggy mattress made of rags that I had placed in the corner of the living room, I sat by him and cried a lot. It took me a long time to recover. Then, three months later, when I was walking back home from the bus stop—after waiting two hours for a bus that never came—I found an abandoned cutie, white with black spots, just walking on the street. A mutt. She approached me, barked once, and wagged her tail.

"You are hungry, aren't you?" I asked, watching her bony body. The moment I saw Motica —the name I gave her— I realized how much we needed each other.

Motica sits next to me when I play my electric piano. When I do, I think of my brother, who, with significant sacrifice, sent it to me from the United States. Whenever I complete a new musical arrangement for my band, I dedicate it to him.

I am a composer and a director, and our group is quite popular with tourists. Our lead singer says she is my age, but I don't believe her. She looks twenty years younger, hardly has any wrinkles, and possesses dance moves that most people our age can't replicate. I would break a bone or two if I tried them. She also possesses an extraordinary talent for singing. Alegría (Happiness). That's her name and the name of the band. It is an ironic name, if you ask me, given the number of people who feel miserable living on this island.

Alegría, the person, and I are best friends. We are both half-cup-full people. It's not as if feeling sorry for us will resolve anything. So we often laugh at her leaky roof on rainy days, the frequent electrical blackouts, our crumbling city, and the endless lines to buy food, sometimes ending in fist-fights.

In some parts of Havana, people know not to walk under balconies as a handful have died, crushed under the weight of falling debris due to the state of disrepair. I, for one, stay away from old buildings. I don't even like visiting friends who live in Old Havana for fear of getting killed. One thing is not taking life seriously, and quite another is to be exposing myself to a sure death.

My acquaintances might say that my life is better than most people's on the island because of my relationships with the tourists who come to see our shows. I must be getting a reputation with them because some, during their multiple trips to Havana, ask me to give them piano lessons.

The incredible power of music.

Tourists don't need to understand my Spanish, nor do I, whatever language they speak. But music—that language is universal.

I can only imagine what it must be like to be a tourist. I see their smiles when they dance to our contagious tunes, some holding *mojitos* and some laughing aloud as if they have had too many drinks. Based on Cuban standards, we consider most tourists rich compared to the average Cuban citizen. So, I feel both admiration and resentment toward them. I'm also grateful for their tips and the care packages a few of them occasionally send me—mostly food.

For the people here, the first level of Maslow's Hierarchy of Needs (breathing, food, water, sex, sleep, homeostasis, and excretion) is all they will ever achieve. The top two levels of esteem and self-actualization are privileges that only those at prominent levels of government can attain.

My relationship with tourists reminds me of the unlikely friendship between Charles Chaplin and Albert Einstein. Einstein told Chaplin he admired him because of the universality of his art. Chaplin replied, "True. But your glory is even greater! The entire world admires you, even though they don't understand a word of what you say."

I don't have a fraction of the talent of Chaplin and Einstein. I hope to leave a mark on the world through my music. Isn't making others happy through music worth something? Tourists admire me only because of the melodies I create in a familiar language that breaks down walls of misunderstanding and even heals. Although Cubans don't understand what some tourists say, they admire their success, the success that allows them to come to the island, buy food and drinks at ridiculous prices, and dance without a care in the world.

Will I ever be able to experience life the way they do?

My friends have told me that it is too late for me. Still, I keep dreaming. There is nothing wrong with that. Is there?

I have simple tastes. Nothing is better than standing on my balcony and looking at the streets with a cup of café con leche. Now, you will never see me with only coffee. I must be the only Cuban on the island who does not appreciate a cup of espresso in the morning. I prefer to dilute it in milk.

That is, whenever I can afford to buy milk. Luckily, my cousin Tania, who lives in the United States, sends me food occasionally. She always knows to send me powdered milk, soya oil, eggs, and any meat on sale. One day, she sent me a handful of steaks. When the delivery man called me to tell me what she had sent, I almost had a heart attack. Well, not really. I tend to exaggerate. But I had not enjoyed a steak in years. And I appreciate a good steak with sauteed onions and fresh garlic. You should've seen me. I had never run downstairs as fast as I ran that day!

"Milagros, where are you going? Slow down! You're going to break a bone!" Lola, a neighbor about my age, said the moment she saw me.

"My cousin sent me some steaks!" I shouted.

I didn't stop to see her reaction but imagined she opened her eyes wide. After all, steak is a luxury for most Cubans.

So, as you come with me on my life journey through Havana, first feast on a big steak and think of me, that is, if you are not a vegetarian. Also, wear a hard hat and watch for falling debris.

Chapter 2

My Unlikely Birth

I don't know why my mother told me about how I came to be. I wouldn't have shared this information with my child if I had been in her position. It was such a shock for me to hear about it. It's a good thing I was born with a suitable defense mechanism: my adaptable personality. It allows me to discard things that hurt me and carry on, seemingly without a care.

So, here is what she told me.

My mother, a tall and shapely woman with short-stylish hair and a hardened expression, was a hypochondriac. One day, she started hearing these horrible noises inside her head. They wouldn't stop. To no avail, she had gone to doctors and even a psychiatrist.

If you have never lived in Cuba, you might not understand what happened next, but I will try to explain it. Many Cubans believe in *Santeria*. Santeria is a fusion of two religions, African and Catholic, which melds African-inspired ritualistic worship and sacrifice and petitions to Catholic saints. Its believers develop intimate relationships with saints, such as *Santa Bárbara* and *San Lázaro,* and offer sacrifices and make promises to them whenever they have problems that no one else can resolve. So, that is precisely what my mother did.

When the noises persisted, my mother went to the *Santuario de San Lázaro*, founded in 1917 in Havana's small town of El Rincón, a church and a hospital-house for leprosy patients. Every December 17, this sanctuary becomes a place of pilgrimage for all believers, which has turned it into an essential element of the Cuban heritage and culture.

Once my mother arrived at this sacred temple, kneeling before *San Lázaro*, she made a promise.

"If you take these noises away, my next child will be named after you."

Mind you, my mother was already in her mid-forties, wore an IUD, and didn't let my father get near her during ovulation. So, it is likely that she thought this wasn't much of a promise, as she was undoubtedly at the end of her childbearing days. But, as my aunts used to say, "God works in mysterious ways."

The noises disappeared two weeks after my mother visited the sanctuary, and happiness returned to our home. Then, three months later, she began to feel weak and would vomit almost every morning.

"It's all in your head," my father—a thin man with small, kind eyes and a receding hairline—would tell her. He had a soft, endearing voice that made me feel safe.

"No, it's not. This is real," she said.

So, she paid a visit to the clinic. After a few tests, the doctor, a man in his early sixties, said, "All your symptoms will end in a few months."

My Unlikely Birth

Wide-eyed, my mother looked at him. He was a man of science, not a fortune teller. How did he know?

"How do you know what is going to happen in a few months from now?"

"By then, you will give birth to a child, and all your problems will end."

Overcome by sadness, she burst into tears.

"What's wrong?" he asked.

"I have been so careful. I also had a device inside me. How could it be?"

"It happens," he said. "It is God's will."

Feeling like she was carrying the world's weight on her shoulders, my mother went home. A couple of hours later, when my father returned from work dressed in his chef uniform, my mother greeted him in the dining room with droopy shoulders and a "someone-died" expression.

"What's wrong?" he asked, touching her shoulders.

"You won't believe this," she replied. "My life is over!"

After delivering the news, his reaction did not match her expectations. He beamed, warmly embraced her, and kissed her.

"I'm going to be a father! I'm going to be a father," he kept repeating like a scratched record.

"Why are you so happy?" she asked, but before he could answer, she added, "Of course you are happy! It's me who will carry this child. It's me who will endure labor pains. How insensitive can you be?"

"I'm sorry, my love. All we can do is to love this gift from God."

My Unlikely Birth

Over the next few months, my mother cried almost every day about her misfortune. She didn't consider me a gift but a punishment. So she went on about her days as if she weren't pregnant. She even shoveled dirt in the backyard to plant fruits and vegetables, hoping the extra effort would result in a miscarriage. But I held on for dear life and came to the world when she was only eight months pregnant.

By the time of my birth, at *La Quinta Dependiente* in the heart of Havana, my mother had already forgotten about her promise. And when the doctor delivered me and announced I was a girl, he asked my mother for my name. But she said she had not thought of one yet.

The doctor then tried to make me cry. He and the young nurse, she in her all-white attire and he in his white coat, exchanged glances. The doctor shook his head. She looked down. My mother then knew something was wrong. Despite the doctor's four attempts to make me cry, I didn't. So he left me for dead in a little bassinet near my parents. His eyes then focused on the granite floor.

"Why isn't she crying?" my father shouted, his eyes full of emotions.

The doctor shook his head and inhaled a big gulp of air.

"I'm sorry. There is nothing I can do," he said.

"Juana!" my father shouted at my mother. "You made a promise to San Lázaro. You were going to give our child his name."

She opened her eyes wide.

My Unlikely Birth

"I had forgotten," she replied. "That's right. Her name will be Lázara Ramona."

"Lázara Ramona?" my father asked.

"My aunt was afraid I was going to lose the pregnancy, so she promised *San Ramón* that if my child were to live, I would name him after him."

Few people in my neighborhood knew the story of Saint Ramón Nonato, who had been extracted from the womb of his deceased mother in Catalunya, Spain, in the XIII century. After dedicating his short life to converting men to Christianity and helping others, he became known as the patron saint of pregnant women.

After my mother explained the reason for my name, my father inhaled, overcome by sadness. "Well, I guess we won't be able to fulfill either promise," he said, wiping the tears off his face with his white handkerchief.

That was when a miracle happened. At least, that is how my parents and even the doctor interpreted it. I started to move my arms and legs and began to cry.

"Dear God,'" my father said, dumbfounded. "She shall be named Lázara Ramona Milagros." (*Milagros* means "miracles" and is a typical girl's name in my culture).

And that was how I came to be. I was the only child in our neighborhood with three names, but everyone would call me "Milagros." Thank God that other relatives did not make more promises, or I might've had the names of every saint in Cuba! It was bad enough that in addition to my three names, I had two last names. That's because in Cuba, like in Spain and other countries in South

11

America, the child's first last name is the father's and the second the mother's. The mother's last name is not discarded like in other countries. In Cuba, women also do not take their husbands' last names like in the United States and most of Japan.

A friend of my mother said that I had two musical names, "Lázara" and "Milagros," two names that contain La, one of the musical notes (do, re, mi, fa, so, *la,* ti).

He predicted that music would run through my veins like water runs through a river, but my parents didn't believe him.

Not at first.

My father and my brother Alfredo

My brother Alfredo and me – 1955 above and my
mother on the next page.

Chapter 3

Chocolate

My arrival into the world made a second person unhappy: my brother Alfredo, who had just turned eight before my birth. I didn't know how he felt at first. After all, I didn't understand how siblings were supposed to act. Then, when I was six, I compared how Berta and Laura, Aunt Angelita's daughters, behaved with each other. Unlike my brother, who ignored me if I tried to play with him, Berta and Laura were always together and seemed to enjoy each other's company. So, I gave up trying to play with my brother and wondered if something was wrong with me.

Luckily, our two-story house, located in the Mantilla neighborhood in the municipality of Arroyo Naranjo south of downtown Havana, was big enough to give each of us our space. My father had built it for my mother, and both prided themselves in that it was the second most beautiful house in the neighborhood, the prettiest being the one that belonged to the owner of the bodega, Odilio. Although, if you asked my mother, she would always tell you ours was the nicest.

Our neighborhood was considered undesirable because of the number of low-income families living in it. Still, when we resided there, we never had any problems with our neighbors. We lived a quiet life. When we walked throughout Mantilla, its lush green landscapes against the bluest of skies made even the poorest abode look pleasing to the eyes. The best gardeners could not have kept the trees in their gardens the way nature maintained those in my neighborhood, the tall queen palm trees and the *framboyán* trees with enchanting orange flowers in full bloom. The fragrance of jasmine flowers permeated the air and made me think there could not be a better place in the world than my neighborhood.

We owned fruit trees and a vegetable garden that helped my parents feed the family. Unlike other streets in the central section of Havana, ours was not paved. The paved section ended at the corner where we lived, so when it rained, the front of our house became a muddy mess. To get from place to place, neighbors had to jump from rock to rock if they were lucky enough to find one nearby.

Sitting on the front porch on rainy days and watching the people try to walk over the mud-covered street was entertaining. I wouldn't say I liked it when someone fell, even less when an older person lost their balance and ended up flat in the mud. If this ever happened, I would rush outside to help them, although not always successfully. I would then get in trouble when I returned home with soiled clothes. But what could I do? Both my parents had taught me to respect and care for older adults. If we saw them standing in a bus and we were sitting, we had to get up and give them our seats. If they were having trouble crossing the street, our moral obligation was to help them.

And talking about older people, I loved going to visit my grandmother Reimunda, who lived with Aunt Angelita and her family in the Santos Suarez neighborhood, only about 6.5 kilometers away, that is, if we used *La Calzada de Diez de Octubre* Avenue to get there. Abuela Reimunda, a Spanish immigrant, was the glue of the Gonzalez family, the matriarch that kept it together. She would tell her daughters and anyone who would listen, "There is nothing worse than being an immigrant. When you immigrate, you stop belonging to one place or another. It is like removing a tropical tree and trying to replant it in the desert."

I never understood my grandmother's analogy, but she seemed wise. She also personified kindness, from how she caressed my hair to the pieces of chocolate she kept especially for me. When she looked at me, the glow in her eyes felt like rays of love pouring from inside her.

My grandparents—Abuela Reimunda and Abuelo Mateo—had eight children; only two were born in Spain. The family was never supposed to end up in Cuba. They had planned to go to Argentina, but their ship departed before they arrived at the Port of Cadiz in Spain. The next boat was going to Cuba, so that became their destination.

On the trip to America, their oldest child died of typhoid fever and had to be laid to rest at sea. My grandparents and their remaining child arrived in Cuba in 1902 after Cuba gained its independence from Spain. They worked hard to raise their family, but their best efforts were not enough to lift them out of poverty. Abuelo Mateo died in the 1930s after all the children had grown up and married.

Reimunda's children remained close as the family grew. So there was always a gathering, a birthday, a baptism, or a wedding. If anyone ever ended up in the hospital, I always felt bad for the nurses and the hospital staff because we would flood the waiting room with our big family. One day, one of the nurses referred to us as *"los muchos"* (the many). However, despite having such a big family of many cousins and aunts and being the youngest of the group, sometimes I felt a bit like an outsider, especially when I learned that my brother was not the only person who disliked me.

So, let me go back to my brother. One day, when my parents left me under his care for a few minutes to go to the grocery store down the street, he said as we both stood on the front porch, "You probably know that I don't like you."

"Why not? What did I do to you?"

"You are an intruder. Do you know what that means?"

I shook my head. But he didn't care to explain it.

I was seven then. Although I didn't know the meaning of that word, I assumed it wasn't good based on how he crumpled his face. Then I noticed that my cousins, Berta and Laura— Aunt Angelita's daughters—didn't like me either. When they visited our house, Berta ignored me. Laura, the oldest, treated Alfredo as her younger brother but looked at me like one looks at a pet. I was just a cute little girl who smelled like *Agua de Violetas* cologne and had bows on her head, a girl who wore the pretty dresses my aunt Angelita made.

I overheard that part of their resentment stemmed from the preferential treatment they thought my mother gave me. Since I was little, I wouldn't say I liked to eat much, but I loved chocolate, a luxury back then. My mother would buy me chocolate and hide it from everyone else. Only I was allowed to eat it.

"Why can't I get a piece?" my brother would ask.

"Your sister is small and thin and doesn't like many foods. But she likes chocolate."

"But I like it too!" he protested.

"Be a good brother and stop whining," she replied.

Alfredo told our cousins. So, they, too, became resentful. One day, when Laura and Berta visited us, the chocolate my mother had put away for me went missing.

When my mother noticed it, like an angry bull, she closed the dining room cabinet where it was hidden.

"Alfredo, where is your sister's chocolate?" she shouted.

"Why do you think it was me?"

"You like chocolate, and I told you it was for your sister."

"I didn't eat her stupid chocolate. Stop blaming me!"

My mother then asked our cousins if they had taken it. This caused an argument with Aunt Angelita.

"Are you accusing my daughters of stealing?"

"No, I'm just asking who took it."

Laura and Berta denied having taken it, and the disappearance of the chocolate remained a mystery until many years later.

Chapter 4

One of the Boys: 1958

In 1958, when I was seven, events unfolded in Havana and throughout the island that would forever change life as we knew it. The revolutionaries used every tactic to ensure their victory against the Fulgencio Batista government, from bombings to destruction of property to the burning of sugar cane fields. But I was too young to care about such things.

My biggest challenge as a child was fighting boredom. What would I do if my parents did not own a television set? Reading a book could have occupied my time, but none in my house interested me. However, a woman named Felicia, one of our neighbors, owned a black and white television, so she invited all the children on our block to watch cartoons at her house. Not that she did this because she wanted to see her home full of children. She, an entrepreneur par excellence, would sell us *durofrío* (shaved ice), candy, and other goodies she made, so we all enjoyed going there. It was like going to a birthday party, except for the payment part.

Although my mother allowed me to watch cartoons at Felicia's house, probably because my brother Alfredo came with me, I seldom had friends over to the house. My mother didn't like many girls my age who lived in our neighborhood. There was always a reason she made up. "I don't trust her parents." "I don't want anyone stealing my things." "I can play with you. You don't need friends to come here."

If I ever wanted to play with dolls or *las casitas* (house), my mother would place my dolls or my tea set on the dining room table and ask me to play with her. Who plays at home with their mother?

"I don't want to play with you. I want to play with my friends," I said.

"Alfredo, why don't you play with your sister?" my mother would tell my brother when she saw me sitting in a rocking chair, kicking my orthopedic shoes together, with an expression of boredom on my face.

"She's a girl!" my fifteen-year-old brother would tell her. "She should play with dolls. I'm a boy! I'm not going to play with girls!"

She would tell him another time, but he protested again, and that was the end of the discussion. So, I would stand on the front porch and look at the empty lot across the street, where my brother and his friends played baseball or marbles. I watched them for hours. One boy had a bat, another would throw him the ball, and the first boy would hit it with the bat. It seemed so easy, so I started practicing on my own. When the boys stopped playing and returned home, I would go to the lot across the street with my brother's bat. I threw the ball up in the air and hit it with the bat. I also practiced running and throwing.

I even learned to play with marbles and roller skates like the boys. One day, when the boys were playing, I went outside and asked one of the older ones if he would allow me to play. They all laughed at me.

"You're a girl," several shouted. I crossed my arms and pouted.

"What are you doing out here? I'm going to tell Mom. Go back inside," Alfredo shouted from across the field.

"I want to play!" I yelled. "I can guarantee you that I'm better than you."

"Oh! She is a feisty one!" one of the boys said. "Alfredo, why don't you let her play? It would be fun to see her fail."

"I don't want to play with a girl, especially my little sister."

"Let her play!" other boys shouted.

My brother shook his head and threw his ball against the ground. It hit a small rock and bounced into the air. Another boy came running and caught it.

"I'm not playing with her," Alfredo said. "If you want to do it, go ahead. I'll sit here and watch her fail."

That made me angry. I had to show him I could be as good as he was. He would not deter me from trying.

One boy handed me the bat. Another positioned himself a few feet away, and everyone occupied their positions on the improvised baseball field.

One of the Boys: 1958

When the pitcher threw me the first ball, it was too high, so I didn't attempt to hit it. His smirk told me he did it on purpose.

"Ball," someone shouted.

"Come on. It would be best if you struck her out!" another boy howled.

The pitcher laughed at me. "I'll get you!" he assured me.

I took a big gulp of the morning air, positioned myself as I had seen the boys do, and kept my eye on the ball. I needed to show them. I couldn't fail.

I watched the pitcher raise his arm in the air, rotate his body, and throw the ball. I waited for it, watching it as it approached, and swung the bat with all my strength. I hit the ball hard, and it flew across the air through center field and beyond.

"Home run!" someone shouted.

"Run to the base," another boy screamed, so I ran until I arrived home.

Alfredo kicked the dirt with his shoes. He looked upset. Why wasn't he happy for me?

"I'm going home," he said.

"Come on, man. Stay. She's good. She is outstanding."

The boys gathered around me and asked me who had taught me.

"I taught myself by watching you play," I said.

I gained the boys' respect and was no longer alone from that day forward.

Chapter 5

Meeting My Idol - 1958

Before the iconic black singer Celia Cruz became popular on the island and all over the world, another singer rose to fame. She was Celeste Mendoza, the queen of *Guaguancó* (street rumba). She was a *mulata* from the province of Oriente with a shapely body, a golden voice, and an extensive repertoire of songs, from Cuban *sones* to *guaracha*.

While Celia Cruz became known as *La Guarachera de Cuba*, Celeste Mendoza gained the name *"la mulata del sabor* (the mulatta of flavor). She performed regularly at *El Cabaret Parisién* at the Hotel Nacional, where my father worked, and on television, and I came to believe that my father was infatuated with her. He was always talking about her. When he did, he became a different person. He would raise his normally quiet voice and wave his hands as he glowed about her stellar performances and their frequent conversations.

Every year, the upper management at the Hotel Nacional invited workers and their families to a big show. Celeste Mendoza performed for the workers surrounding the hotel's large swimming pool. I used to love going to those annual shows. In 1958, as we prepared to attend that year's party,

26

my father asked me, "Do you want to meet Celeste Mendoza?"

Wide-eyed, I nodded my head enthusiastically. I was enthralled by show business—dancing, lights, costumes, hair, and makeup—and the music that always got into my soul.

"Are you her friend?" I asked even though I knew the answer.

"Yes, we are terrific friends. She always comes over before her show, and she talks to me. She is a truly kind person," he said.

My mother gave him an angry look. She pursed her lips and folded her arms. If stares could kill, my mother's, intense and threatening, would have destroyed him at that very moment. But luckily, it didn't. Like a ferocious she-wolf, she let out an enraged huff.

"What's the big deal with that woman? Are you in love with her or something?" she asked.

My father smiled and walked toward my mother with his arms wide open. As he embraced her, he asked, "Are you jealous?"

"No, I'm not jealous!" she protested and pulled herself away from him. But I could tell she wasn't being truthful.

That night, my father looked so handsome in his white, long-sleeve guayabera shirt, while Mamá wore a long beige dress that her sister Angelita had made for her.

"So Papi, can I meet her and say hello?"

"Why do you want to meet her?" my brother asked.

"I want to be like her!" I said.

"You don't know what you want," he said. He was always giving me a tough time.

"Don't bother your sister," my father told my brother. "Of course, you can talk to her."

I was so excited.

That night, as the warm breeze from the Caribbean Sea caressed my hair, I listened to Celeste Mendoza and immersed myself in her world and her music. Nothing else mattered that night. Her voice was perfection personified.

I knew then that I wanted nothing more than to belong to that world. But how?

The night was everything I thought it would be: dance, music, singing, lights, and the sweet aroma of Cuban food. At the end of the performance, my father took me by the hand.

"Juana, stay here with Alfredo. I will be right back."

We disappeared into the crowd. I didn't know where we were going because everyone around me was taller than me. I kept my eyes on the ground, admiring all the fancy shoes men and women wore and smelling their fruity or musky perfumes.

"Celeste!" I heard my father say.

"Hey! You made it!" I heard her say.

"I wouldn't miss it for the world," he replied. "You are the queen of this island."

I saw her standing in front of me. She didn't have a pretty face, but her smile made her look bigger than life. It was as if an angel were standing in front of me. An angel who was now devoting her full attention to me.

"And who is this pretty girl?" she asked, caressing my hair.

"This is Milagros!" my father said proudly, pulling me toward her. I shrugged, not knowing what to do or how to act in front of my idol.

"Hello, my love," she said with a sweet voice.

"She wants to be like you when she grows up," he said.

She bent down and spoke in my ear.

"And I am sure that you will be famous one day. All you must do is believe it. It's that easy."

I could feel my face turning red. I looked down, not knowing how to act.

"She's shy," my father said.

"That will change. You'll see."

That was the best night of my life. A small fire ignited within me that breezy evening, and I sensed that this encounter would change my life.

Chapter 6

Playing by Ear - 1958

On this sunny Saturday morning, I was sitting on the floor in the corner of our small but spotless dining room in the house that my father had built in the Mantilla neighborhood. In front of me stood an empty round can of about two feet in diameter, turned upside down, and I made music by hitting its flat surface with sticks.

All the windows were open, and the sun filtered through the one closest to me, making part of our square dining room table glow.

From where I sat, I could see my mother cooking black beans and rice in the kitchen, making the house smell like a mixture of onions, garlic, oregano, and tomato sauce. I wondered if she knew how much I despised them. I liked any other beans: red, white, even garbanzo. She made black beans so often—probably because they were easy to make—and I got tired of them. And they did a number on my stomach.

"Milagros, for the love of God, stop making noises!" my mother yelled.

Despite my mother's objections to my musical expression, I played with more determination when I heard her complain. I didn't know why I enjoyed seeing her all worked up about the minor things.

My long, black hair bounced as I rhythmically moved my head back and forth.

Sitting in a rocking chair in the living room reading the most recent issue of Bohemia magazine, my father rose from his seat and walked toward me. He stood before me wearing a white T-shirt, beige pants, and brown flip-flops and applauded me, and his eyes shone with pride.

"It's not noise, Juana," my father replied. "It sounds rather nice."

"What is she going to do next? Dance like the dancers at Tropicana Cabaret?"

"And what's wrong with that? If our daughter likes music and the arts, shouldn't we support her? Her music teacher talked to me the other day when I went to pick her up. He told me that Milagros has an exceptional ear for music. He caught her sitting by the piano and playing a tune she heard him play. She doesn't know how to read music yet and can replicate anything she hears. That's a gift!"

"What will you tell me next, that you want to buy her a piano?"

"You read my mind. That is exactly what I plan to do," my father replied. He was soft-spoken, in contrast with my mother's boisterous outbursts.

My mother wore the metaphorical pants in the house and was a couple of inches taller than my father (when she wore heels). Most of the time, he allowed her to win the arguments and walked away, but he stayed firm regarding my musical development.

"Have you lost your mind?" she asked. "How much is a piano?"

"I checked. It is 250 pesos."

"That's too much money!" she said.

"I am a chef and manage the kitchen in one of the most important hotels in the city," he added as he walked toward the kitchen. "It's not easy to work at the Hotel Nacional. It takes special mindfulness and skill to please tourists. I make good money. What better way to use it than to support our daughter?"

My mother let out an exasperated grunt.

"It's not like I don't work. Unlike other women who stay at home, I contribute to the household, even if I don't make as much as you."

My mother worked at the shoe factory Ingelmo, making perforations on men's shoes, which was immensely popular in the 1950s.

"Let's not make this a discussion about money," he said. "I told you that you don't have to work. You can stay at home with our daughter. I want us to agree on this. Let's buy her a piano. Okay, my love?"

They remained silent for a moment. Then he placed his arms around her and tried to kiss her. She pushed him away and shouted, "Stop trying to make me change my mind by hugging and kissing me!"

Giggling, he asked, "Is it working?"

She waved her arms in the air.

"Fine! Do whatever you want, but when she gets bored of playing, we'll see what you do with the piano."

Playing by Ear - 1958

And that was the start of my journey as a pianist. My father bought me a used upright piano, a Baldwin a coworker was selling. It was so heavy, but my father and his friends from work dragged it inside the house and placed it in a corner of the living room, across from two rocking chairs.

I played by ear for hours. At first, only my father would sit in a rocking chair and listen to me. But after a few weeks, even my mother noticed my talent.

She would come from the kitchen, dry her hands on her pink apron, and ask me, "What was that you were playing?"

"It's a song by Sebastian Bach that I heard my piano teacher play. I don't know its name."

Later, I would learn that I had been playing Bach's Minuet in G Major. I would also understand that, although this minuet was attributed to Johann Sebastian Bach, it was actually written by Christian Petzold.

So, I continued to take piano lessons, from classical music to Cuban standards. There was nothing I heard that I couldn't replicate in the piano. The piano became an extension of my being, a way to express my happiness or frustrations, and the means of stepping into the future that awaited me.

Chapter 7

Growing Up

On January 1, 1959, when I was almost eight, an event occurred that would eventually change my family's life. That morning, when we woke up, Cuba had no president. The night before, while people welcomed the arrival of a new year by dancing, drinking, and throwing a bucket of water out the front door (a Cuban tradition), President Fulgencio Batista and his family fled the island.

As the news spread throughout the nation, people took to the streets waving Cuban flags to celebrate the victory of Fidel Castro's rebels.

My family became divided overnight; some supported Castro, and others were skeptical of his promises.

On April 19, 1959, Fidel Castro appeared on "Meet the Press" during his visit to the United States and stated that he was not a communist. That made those people in the family who opposed him more comfortable. However, in 1961, as the relationship between the United States and Cuba deteriorated, he proclaimed himself a Marxist-Leninist. I would hear conversations over the dinner table about what this meant.

Marx and Lenin were clearly communists, and I didn't understand how Castro could so quickly change his mind. However, I didn't know much about communism and what it could do to a country. I asked my parents, but they said children should not get involved in politics.

Imagine what Castro's declaration did to his supporters, including those in my family. They felt betrayed. So, in the years that followed, my parents lost many of their relatives and friends to exile. People were leaving by the thousands, but my mother kept remembering what our grandmother Reimunda had said about the life of an immigrant.

"There is nothing worse than being an immigrant. When you immigrate, you stop belonging to one place or another. It is like removing a tropical tree and trying to replant it in the desert."

Despite these warnings, my cousins Laura and Berta wanted to leave Cuba, but their mother, Angelita, and her husband were too unhealthy to follow their daughters. So, Laura and Berta delayed their plans. My mother talked to them to convince them to stay. She didn't want them to leave. Laura was one of her favorite nieces, the kindest and sweetest. Berta, however, was too much like my mother, stubborn and determined like her.

Laura and Berta said they had no choice. They had promised their mother Angelita that they would leave Cuba one day.

Several of Aunt Isidora's eight children also left. Aunt Isidora became so distraught about her children's departure that she tried to take her life. I didn't know this until years later because news like this wasn't shared with the children.

It saddened Mom to learn that Aunt Lucinia was also leaving. And just like that, little by little, our family members became separated by the Caribbean Sea, like cotton flecks or particles of dust in the wind.

"I don't care what the rest of the family does," my mother said, even though we knew how sad this made her. "You and your brother were born here, and you will die here."

My brother and I didn't say anything. What did we know about politics or what would happen next?

Chapter 8

Hotel Nacional

For many years, the Hotel Nacional, the massive structure built in 1930 facing the seafront of the Vedado District, was my father's pride and joy. His eyes sparkled when he told family and friends about his responsibilities at what he called "the best hotel in Cuba."

The hotel had been designed by the prestigious firm McKim, Mead, & White, the architects of Columbia University in New York City and the Boston Public Library. From the outside, it looked remarkably like The Breakers in Palm Beach, Florida. Over the years, it hosted the Hollywood elite and foreign diplomats.

In June 1960, everything changed.

I don't remember what day my father came home with the news, but I recall his expression. When I hugged him, he seemed worried and pensive, and unlike other days, he didn't ask me about my day at school. He inhaled after he kissed my mother on the cheek and asked her to go to the bedroom. He had something to share with her. Judging by the line between his eyes and his seriousness, I knew something big had happened. So when my father closed the door, I quietly stood in front of it with my ear pressed to it.

"Fidel Castro nationalized the hotel industry," he said. I didn't know what "nationalized" meant, but I soon understood.

"Who is going to manage the hotel?" she asked.

"The government."

"And what do they know about running hotels?"

He remained quiet.

"They know nothing about it," he finally replied.

"Oh, my God!" my mother exclaimed. "What will happen with your job?"

"Someone still needs to direct the kitchen," he said.

"So why do you seem so concerned?"

"I just don't know if I made the right decision," he said. "I guess time will tell."

He proceeded to tell my mother what had occurred.

The hotel directors had met with my father before they left Cuba.

"Angelito," one of them said. "We want you and your family to come with us. We have a job for you at one of the best hotels in Puerto Rico."

My father remembered what my mother had shared with him about the life of an immigrant. His family had roots in Cuba, and he couldn't just leave.

"I appreciate the offer," he said, "but everything I know is here, including the house I built for my family. I cannot just start at zero again. You understand."

The director expressed his disappointment and wished him luck.

When my father responded, he never anticipated that the family he wanted to protect would soon be fractured by the same elements who had taken over the hotel.

Chapter 9

Visiting Alfredo

In 1960, Alfredo told my parents he wanted to study agricultural accounting outside Havana. My mother wasn't happy.

"Our son is becoming a man. We didn't raise him for us and must let him go," my father told her in his usual calm and low tone.

"But no one can take care of him the way I do," she replied, scrunching her eyebrows and giving my father a worried look.

At first, I thought it would be nice not to have him around looking at me as if I had a giant bump on my head, but I soon realized I was fooling myself.

I turned ten on January 15, 1961. By then, Alfredo had already left home. That day, my parents bought me a vanilla cake with pink frosting and sang *Happy Birthday* in a gloomy ceremony that failed to make me feel better than when I was nine. No other children were present, which made my brother's absence even more noticeable.

For the first time, I realized I missed my brother.

We had always given each other a tough time, and he looked at me as an intruder. Now that I understood that term after asking my teacher what it meant, it was easier to grasp why he resented me. After my birth, he no longer had my parents' full attention. He thought I had taken half of his time with our parents away. I wouldn't have felt the same if I had been the oldest sibling. But like Grandmother Reimunda used to say, "You cannot judge someone unless you have walked in their shoes." Regardless of how I would have acted, something was true. A part of me was missing, and I couldn't wait to see him again.

My mother told me he was staying near the mountains of the province of Oriente, in the eastern part of the island. Even though we were about 750 kilometers away (466 miles), to me, he was in another part of the world.

I didn't know that those who had fled the country and many people within Cuba disagreed with the revolution. My parents had kept me away from the televised executions, the massive jailing of opponents, and anything that would have disrupted my innocent view of the world. So, you can imagine my surprise when radio and television stations announced that Cuba was under attack.

On April 17, 1961, a group of exiles known as Brigade 2506 landed on the beaches along the Bay of Pigs. The country was immediately mobilized. My parents feared for my brother, whose classes immediately changed from agricultural accounting to military tactics aimed at deploying him and other students to fight near *Ciénaga of Zapata* (Zapata Swamp). I could sense the tension at my house until the fighting ended on April 20, 1961, and my mother learned that my brother did not have to be deployed. Brigade 2506, as small as it was, inflicted severe damage. However, after not receiving the air support that the United States promised, the exiles were quickly outnumbered and had no choice but to turn themselves in. I didn't know about all the people who were jailed and questioned during that time or about the over one hundred who were killed. I would learn about that years later.

In the months after my brother's departure, my piano playing became more melancholic. Channeling my feelings through my music was better than telling my mother how much I missed my obnoxious brother. I didn't want her to call me weak and sentimental. I could have told my father, but that would not have resolved anything. Alfredo was gone, and that was that.

A week before Mother's Day, my mother announced, "We are going to Oriente to see your brother!"

My eyes lit up when she told me.

"Really?" I asked.

"Why do you look so happy if he always gave you such a hard time?" she asked.

I shrugged.

But after her declaration, I felt energized and started to play more lively tunes. I went from *boleros* to *mambo* and *cha-cha-cha*. I even caught my parents dancing to my music in the living room.

I counted the days and hours until our upcoming trip. At last, on the Saturday before Mother's Day, we left Havana on an interprovincial bus. I was so excited! It was the first time I had left our province. At the time, we only had six provinces, plus the island of Isla de Pinos, so this trip would allow us to see most of the country, except for Pinar del Rio (the province west of Havana) and Isla de Pinos. Years later, the six provinces would divide into fourteen.

As was customary for travel in the years before the revolution, my parents dressed like they were attending church. My father wore a suit, and my mother wore an elegant dress that Aunt Angelita had made for her. Although I was ten, I had to wear a ribbon on my head, a pink girly dress, white dressy socks, and black patent shoes. Luckily, we did not wait until July to make this trip. The bus was not air-conditioned, and although our windows were open, it would get warm inside, especially when it wasn't moving.

After the first two hours of our trip, my mother dozed off, but my eyes stayed fixed on the view from my window. It was true that we lived in a semi-rural area, but nothing compared to the unrestrained beauty of Cuba's countryside.

I inhaled the morning's dew-infused air and watched the extensive plains dotted by queen palms, shrubs, and bright orange *Framboyán* trees. As I contemplated the colorful birds chirping and flying by, the cloudless blue skies, and the thriving green fields, I wondered if José Martí, a national hero and poet, had found inspiration in some places we traveled.

Cuba's fields were ideal for writers and poets. They were visual songs composed by nature itself.

During our trip, my father was a wealth of information. It was as if I were traveling with my human databank. He told me about the Escambray mountain range in central Cuba, one of the Caribbean's most picturesque, perfect for bird watchers and nature lovers. He talked about its caves. He didn't tell me about the Escambray rebellion, which involved groups of insurgents hidden in these mountains to fight against Castro's government. Many would end up in jail or executed.

He spoke about the colonial city of *Trinidad*, with its well-kept Spanish architecture, and the *Topes de Collantes* mountains, with its famous 62-meter-high *Salto de Caburní* waterfall.

During the years leading up to our trip, I attended a primary school that was only available for children of La Ruta Cuatro (Route Four) transportation workers. My father didn't work in transportation but, through his connections, managed to send me there. That school gave me a good education, but nothing compared with what I learned during our trip to Oriente.

This trip left me wanting to see other parts of the world, like my idol, Celeste Mendoza, had done. I hoped that my chosen profession would open the doors to that world that seemed so out of reach.

When we arrived at our destination, the City of Holguín, one of the largest in Cuba, we walked to a small hotel called Los Angeles. By then, the sun had vanished from the sky, and I could hear crickets outside our hotel. Until 1976, this city was part of the Province of Oriente. Then, it became a province. We freshened up and went into the lobby to ask where to eat. A young, tall man overheard us and suggested a nearby Fonda, a family-owned hole-in-the-wall eatery owned by a Spaniard.

Visiting Alfredo

I didn't notice what my parents ordered, but the eggs and white rice I ate didn't stay inside me for long. My vomiting didn't end until the evening, and I fell asleep in a fetal position.

On Sunday, Mother's Day, after having *café con leche* and toast at the same Fonda, we took a long walk toward my brother's school, *Instituto Tecnológico de Holguín*. The place was off the main road, away from everything.

As we approached the building that morning, I saw a very skinny young man with a bushy beard walking in our direction and waving at us. The sun blinded us, so it wasn't easy to see who it was. Then, my father figured it out.

"Alfredo?" he shouted.

"Is that him?" I asked. "My brother is not that skinny and doesn't have a beard. And that boy is much darker than my brother!"

"It is him!" my mother said. "What has happened to my son?"

When Alfredo sprinted toward us, he looked like a skeleton running away from the science class. He first embraced my mother. "Happy Mother's Day, Mamá," he said.

"My good son," she replied, filling him with kisses. "What have they done to you?"

He glanced at me, rubbed my head, and smiled—an unexpected reaction. I didn't know how to react. Then, I said what was on my mind. I didn't want to waste such a long trip by leaving words unsaid.

"I missed you," I said and looked down.

"Come on," he said. "Give your brother a hug."

I hugged him. As we embraced, I saw my mother wipe a tear.

"This is the best Mother's Day present you could have given me," she said.

I didn't know what to make of my brother's reaction. Something in his look told me he wasn't being truthful.

My father was the last one to hug my brother. I could see how he looked at him, a combination of pride and sadness.

That day, Alfredo told us about his experiences at the school. His class was required to climb *El Pico Turquino*, the highest mountain in the Sierra Maestra Mountain range, six times during the class duration. That was a minimum requirement for graduation. I didn't understand why, and when I asked him, he shrugged. He ate little and was exposed to the sun a lot.

My mother asked him about the food they were feeding him. It sounded awful—the white rice was often infected with weevils, the beans had little rocks, and chicken was rarely added. As my brother related his experiences, my mother breathed faster and closed her fists.

"They cannot treat you that way!" she shouted. "I'm going to the administration and demand that they improve the quality of the food they give you!"

"Let it go, Juana," my father said. "You must be careful."

"No one will tell me not to defend my son," she replied. "Not even you!"

My father shook his head. Tensing her face, my mother turned toward my brother and added, "Where is the administration office?"

Nervously, Alfredo pointed to it. Without saying another word, my mother walked hurriedly toward the building. I didn't know how she could walk as fast as she did with her white skirt that reached just below her knees. At least, this morning, she wore her flat shoes. I could only imagine the way she talked to the administrators. My mother had a unique way of compelling others to obey, from her stern voice and determined expression to the urgency of her hand movements as she spoke. She could have been a school principal if she had lived another life.

My mother returned twenty minutes later with a sweaty forehead.

"It's all settled. The food will improve; if it doesn't, you will tell me. You hear me?"

"Yes, Mamá," Alfredo said.

My mother then behaved as if nothing had happened, and we had an enjoyable rest of the day, so much so that I didn't want it to end. That Mother's Day was the most memorable and one of the best days of my life. That is, until right before we left. My brother quietly approached me and whispered, "I still think you're an intruder. Don't let what I did today fool you."

Visiting Alfredo

Our visit to Alfredo

Chapter 10

The Literacy Campaign

M y father was never involved in politics. After working at the hotel all day, he only wished to spend time with his family. My mother thought that he didn't feel Cuban enough because even though he was born in Havana, his parents sent him to Spain to live with his grandparents when he was an infant. He lived there until the Spanish Civil War started, when his grandparents insisted he return to Cuba. They didn't want him to die in a war that had nothing to do with him. He was in his twenties then. But he had seen first-hand what politics could do to a country and wanted no part of it.

As the daughter of a Spanish immigrant, my mother thought it was her obligation to support the new revolutionary government. First, she joined the Federation of Cuban Women. This organization was involved with the Literacy Campaign from 1960 to 1961, aiming to improve literacy while creating a collective identity through politicized educational pamphlets. During this campaign, thousands of educators from the cities were deployed to rural areas for months. Upon returning to Havana, government officials called upon the province's people to provide temporary housing for educators until they returned home.

My mother was the only person in our neighborhood who assisted with this endeavor. The female educator that she chose to house at our home slept on my bed for three days while I took Alfredo's room. My mother fed her and catered to her needs like her daughter. After the young woman went home, my mother found a small bottle of cologne under the pillow that the educator had left her as a gift.

My mother's willingness to help the educators earned her a good reputation in our neighborhood. She hoped that this goodwill would one day benefit her children.

Chapter 11

The Cow

Food shortages became prevalent in Cuba three years after Fidel Castro came to power. Some of my parents' friends blamed the United States embargo, while others claimed internal mismanagement. Others said it was a combination of factors, including the massive exodus and resulting brain drain.

Although my father didn't like politics, he kept himself informed. He explained that President John F. Kennedy had imposed the embargo in February 1962 after Castro aligned himself with the Soviet Union and China and nationalized the assets of United States companies operating in Cuba. My father then learned from speaking with coworkers who had family in the United States that under the embargo, U.S. companies could still export agricultural commodities to Cuba if the Cuban government paid cash in advance. No credit sales were allowed. Some of my father's friends argued that Cuba could have purchased the goods it needed using cash if its internal resources had been appropriately managed.

I was too young to understand these complex matters. All I knew was that my father and mother

51

had opposing views and often argued about who was at fault.

In response to the shortages, on March 12, 1962, each household was given a rationing book called *La Tarjeta de Abastecimiento* that allowed families to buy certain essential foods at subsidized prices. Milk also began to be restricted to children and the elderly. Cubans love a nice cup of *café con leche* in the morning. So, you can imagine the impact of this restriction.

To ensure an adequate supply of milk, my father decided to purchase a cow from an old man from whom he used to buy milk. The man was retiring and told my father he could sell him a pregnant cow at an excellent price. My father was so happy when he brought the cow home. Based on his reading, the cow would start producing milk after giving birth to its first calf.

So, my father taught me how to brush it to keep it clean. I also gave her a name. Matilda. When, after several months, Matilda didn't get any bigger, my father realized that she wasn't pregnant. The seller had lied to him. So, he decided to return the cow and get his money back. I had already become attached to Matilda and didn't take his decision lightly. I cried and begged him to let us keep her. But I stopped when he explained that the family needed the money.

As he walked the cow back to the old man's farm that afternoon, in the opposite direction, another farmer passed by pulling a bull with a leash. Suddenly, the bull turned around, got away from his owner, and started following Matilda. As if feeling threatened, she started running to get away from him. In no time, my father, still holding on to Matilda's leash, was dragged all over the mud while trying to stop her.

An hour after he left, my father returned home looking like he had been wrestling in mud.

"What happened to you?" my mother asked. He told her what happened. As he spoke, my mother tried to remain serious as long as possible. And so did Alfredo—who was back home after finishing his certification—and I. But after a while, she couldn't stop herself and burst into laughter, and we did, too.

"Did you get your money back?" my mother said when she managed to laugh.

"Yes, I did!" he replied angrily.

That was the last time my father bought a cow. In 1963, after Hurricane Flora resulted in the loss of a fifth of the country's cattle, cows became sacred. They could no longer be killed without permission from the government.

Our family had no other option but to adapt to the new rules and hope things didn't worsen. Matilda was now part of history, and so was *café con leche.*

The Cow

Mom -at our backyard in Mantilla

Chapter 12

Becoming a Pianist

After graduation in 1962, Alfredo obtained a job as a director of an agricultural cooperative. Cooperatives were created after 1959 when Fidel Castro's government implemented two agrarian reforms that culminated in the transfer of 70% of farmlands from private owners to the government.

Now that Alfredo had a respectable job, it was time to move on to the next stage of his adult life. In 1963, he met a petite young woman with blondish hair and sparkling brown eyes who was the opposite of him. She was joyful and carefree, the life of the party. In only a few months, he married her.

I don't think my mother liked Anita much at first because she would not allow her to use our only refrigerator after she and Alfredo moved into our home's second floor. It was a constant fight between my mother and Alfredo. You might think I would have enjoyed seeing my mother's anger directed toward him, especially after the way he treated me. But I pitied him. I could imagine how difficult it must have been for him to be in the middle of the two women he loved the most.

In 1965, everything changed when Alfredo and Anita had their first son. Yes, I was finally an aunt, a fourteen-year-old aunt! It was amazing to witness what a grandson did for my mother, how the hardness in her expression melted away when she held the baby boy in her arms.

"Doesn't he look just like his father?" my mother asked often.

"I think he looks like both of us," Alfredo answered.

So my mother would direct her attention to the baby and say childishly, "Your daddy doesn't know what he's talking about. Does he? Of course, you look like your daddy. A carbon copy of him when he was your age."

After that, my house was no longer dull—quite the opposite. Finding peace between the baby's crying and my mother's orders was challenging: "Did you change the baby's diapers?" "Did you bathe the baby?" "Angelito, lower the volume of the radio. You're going to wake up the baby!"

Eight months after his birth, my nephew, Alfredo Jr. (whom we called Alfredito), became enamored with my music, particularly when I played children's songs and taught him how to applaud. I loved seeing my little audience at home grow. Even Anita sat next to her son to watch me play.

***

As I approached my fifteenth birthday celebration, the most important party for a girl growing up in Cuba, Anita took control of the planning. Of course, first, she had to convince my mother that she was too busy with her revolutionary commitments and "duties as our household's matriarch." My mother liked the sound of that.

"That's right," she said. "I am the matriarch of this household. Let no one forget it."

Anita was much more intelligent than my mother thought. She knew exactly what my mother wanted to hear. Of course, my party was a success, with Anita driving the celebrations and my parents providing her with all the support she needed to succeed. The few relatives who remained in Cuba and many neighbors and friends attended it. There was music, a choreographed dance, laughter, cake, and a delicious macaroni salad. And we all danced until midnight.

In 1966, a few months after my fifteenth birthday, I graduated as a proper pianist. My graduation became a big deal at home. My parents were more excited than I had seen them in years. Everyone in the family attended it, including the new baby and the other one on the way.

I was thrilled about my future and all its possibilities. After graduation, my parents sat across from me in the living room and asked me, "Now, what are your plans?"

I felt so grown up when they asked me this. Without hesitation, I said, "I want to be in a musical band."

"Are you sure?" my mother asked.

"Yes. That's what I want."

She agreed to help me obtain the necessary approvals and an employee card that would allow me to get a job. I did not know how she managed to do it. I heard she had to speak to several people. Knowing how resourceful and determined she was, she probably even paid people off to make it happen.

Becoming a Pianist

I was elated when my mother presented me with my official work papers.

With my father's contacts at the hotel and the number of talented artists who had left Cuba, like the renowned singer Celia Cruz, it wasn't difficult for me to secure a job as a pianist. But there was a hurdle I had to get over. I was audience-shy. On top of this, my mother had to come with me to every engagement. She was not about to allow her fifteen-year-old to be alone at bars in the middle of the night, especially when my first job was working as the only female for an all-men band.

I froze the first time I sat before a piano and turned my head toward the sizeable audience-filled auditorium. Suddenly, the years of training became meaningless. I watched the musical sheets before me, and it felt like I had never taken lessons. Everything looked foreign to me.

I looked at José, the bongo player, a black man with kind eyes who quickly would become my best friend and advocate. He recognized the terror in my eyes. He left his post and approached me quietly. He first turned off my microphone and whispered in my ear.

"Everything is going to be fine," he said. This happens to all of us when we first hit the stage. It is called stage fright, and it is perfectly normal. Take a deep breath. Look at the audience and think of something funny. For example, imagine that everyone is naked."

I did as he said. He turned the microphone back on and returned to his post. Then, the weirdest thing happened. I had to cover my mouth because I almost laughed when I saw the audience and imagined they had left their clothes at home. After that, I remembered how to read music and began playing. José glanced at me and nodded in approval. That relaxed me a little. For the rest of the night, I had to resist looking at the spectators, afraid I would start laughing at them.

My mother, watching from the first row, would tell me later that I looked like a star. I was wearing a dress that Aunt Angelita had made for Alfredo's wife. My mother said she could hear audience members comment about my talent. They didn't understand how someone as young as me played as well as I did.

As much as my mother had resisted the idea of me becoming a pianist, she had become my greatest supporter. She no longer worked at the shoe factory, which allowed her to devote her time to me and household chores. Also, Anita was thankful that my job's responsibilities kept my mother away from the house for a few hours a week.

A win-win for everyone.

Chapter 13

My Czech Boyfriend

"Milagros, you should find yourself a nice young man to marry," my mother often told me after my seventeenth birthday.

She even arranged two dates for me. One was a very tall man. I would have injured my neck if I had ever tried to kiss him. The other was shorter and ten years older than me, a guy who loved to speak constantly about himself. After her failed attempts, she stopped trying.

Unlike other girls, I didn't know how to flirt graciously. I could see young women in my neighborhood do it successfully, from the seductive head tossing to the coy smiles. When I tried to imitate them in front of the mirror, I looked awkward, and my moves were unnatural.

Maybe it was my lack of self-esteem. I thought I looked like a *palitroque* (a thin breadstick). I heard that my figure was deemed attractive in the United States, but here in Cuba, men preferred curvy women. Despite my unattractiveness, occasionally, after finishing a performance, a young man would approach me and ask me if he could go out with me. I must confess. I did some strange things when they did.

"You need to ask my parents," I typically replied. I had difficulty saying no. Besides, who in their right mind would come to my house after meeting me only once? To ensure they received the message loud and clear, I would add, "My parents are very strict."

They often walked away, and I never saw them again, but a few daredevils asked for my address and showed up at my house.

The few times this happened, I ran toward the back of the house when I saw them.

"Mamá, can you open the door?" I would shout from the bathroom where I hid, not sure why. "There is a guy here for me. Please tell him I'm not allowed to go out with anyone."

"Why would you give him your address if you had no intentions of going out with him?"

"I thought he would not come," I replied.

"I guess I will never understand you," she replied. I then heard the diminishing sound of her footsteps as she headed for the front door.

At first, my mother helped me with my visitors. Then, one day, she surprised me when, instead of helping me, she shouted, "You asked him to come here; you tell him you don't want to see him! I'm not your messenger."

So much for that idea; after that, when a suitor I didn't find compatible approached me, I gave him an excuse.

I would say, "I'm sorry. I have a boyfriend." But I was a horrible liar.

Honestly, I didn't know what I was looking for. My grandmother Reimunda told me I would know when the right guy came. She said I would not need to practice any moves when that day came. My body alone would do all the right things seamlessly.

I feared that if one day I met that special someone and brought him home, it would end the relationship. I knew my mother would not leave us alone for a single moment.

So I had a few secret dates and did what teenage girls did during those years—lots of kissing but no contact with the sacred parts. Afterward, I always felt guilty, a guilt that my Catholic grandmother had instilled in me. "God knows everything," she used to tell me.

One day, after concluding that I would never find the right person, a young man shyly approached me at the end of my performance at the Sierra Maestra Hotel bar —near the Almendares River. The Sierra Maestra Hotel was in a zone known as La Puntilla. It included two city blocks of buildings that housed foreign technicians who worked on various infrastructure projects. Some technicians lived alone, and others with their families. But later, I learned that this was not one of the technicians who lived at the hotel.

The young man spoke another language. I was twenty-something then and not as shy as before. I raised my palms, then my eyebrows, and replied, "I don't understand." Then I noticed his brown eyes, which complemented his dark hair. He had a kind expression that didn't intimidate me, and he was handsome in a regular way, not overly so.

He brought his index finger to his chin as if he were thinking. Then he said in bad Spanish, "Pretty," and pointed at me and the piano.

Either he considered me pretty, or thought the piano and I were pretty, or liked how I played the piano. I had no idea what he was trying to convey, but I went along with it.

"Thank you," I said.

He smiled genuinely and continued conversing with me with gestures and using the few words he knew. First, he asked me if I was Cuban. I nodded.

"Name?" he asked.

"Milagros.

"Mi-la-gros," he repeated.

I smiled approvingly, "That's right! And you?"

"Adam," he replied joyfully. His smile revealed a standard set of teeth, not too white, like those of North American actors.

"So, where are you from, Adam?" I asked.

"Čechoslovák," he replied in Czech. I understood that because it was not too different from Spanish.

"Are you on vacation?

"Va-ca-tion," he repeated. "Hmm.. oh, prázdniny. Vacation. Prázdniny. No, no vacation. Job."

"So you have a job in Cuba? Strange. What do you do?"

He didn't seem to understand. I pointed at myself and the piano. Then I pointed at him with a questioning expression. His expression finally lit up.

"Engineer, hmmm. Techno electric company near Mariel Port," he said in broken Spanish.

Attractive, kind, and had a job that my mother would approve of. But I thought he was being kind. Soon, he would turn around and leave. That was what I told myself, except that it didn't happen that way. He stayed and kept asking me questions.

After a while, he asked, "Coppelia?" And he pointed at him and me.

I replied slowly, pronouncing each word.

"You want me to go with you to Coppelia? The ice cream parlor?"

"Ice cream, yes," he said happily.

Well, I loved ice cream. It was a public place close to where I was performing. So why not? But it was nighttime, so we agreed to meet at Coppelia the next day at 2 p.m.

That Thursday, I told my mother that my performance was scheduled to start earlier than usual due to a special event. I pretended to be busy when I said this and evaded her eyes. Otherwise, she would have looked right through me. So, I left the house at 1 p.m. and walked toward the bus station.

At almost two, I arrived at the intersection of L and 23 Streets in El Vedado and walked toward *El Coppelia Park*. In the middle of it was the ice cream parlor of the same name. Built in 1966, the domed pavilion was across from the Habana Libre Hotel.

Adam waved at me from the line. I greeted him with a hug and kiss on the cheek, which must have caught him by surprise based on his geeky behavior.

We stood behind a couple with two small children who gave us a curious glance when Adam and I started to communicate. I wondered if they could tell that Adam was not from Cuba. If they didn't at first, they confirmed their suspicion as I kept talking to Adam as if he were deaf.

I will never forget that first date, our easy conversation despite the language barrier, and the delicious strawberry ice cream that tasted better during that visit than any previous time. That date and several that followed proved that my grandmother Reimunda was right.

"Once you find the right man, you will know. You won't have to practice in front of a mirror. You will know exactly what to say and what to do."

My Czech Boyfriend

Adam and I - 1972

Chapter 14

Poland

You might wonder why I was no longer working with a band when I met Adam. It wasn't my objective to become a soloist. I considered it quite dull, in fact, but the situation forced me to do so. I needed to help my parents financially.

After graduating as a pianist, my first job was working with a jazz band. But that wasn't what I wanted. I did it for a few years to gain experience. Then, I found a job working for the *Combo Los Llamas*, a smaller group that performed in nightclubs. Smaller groups were more popular at the time because they could participate in a greater variety of engagements. As part of this group, I appeared on television twice or thrice weekly and at popular places like *El Cabaret Parisién*, where Celeste Mendoza, my idol, used to perform. I also performed at the *Copa Room* at the Riviera and had radio appearances.

I made my first international trip as part of the group *Los Llamas*. I didn't choose where to go or receive additional compensation for traveling to this far-away place. The government sent us there for a couple of weeks as part of their arrangement with the government of Poland.

Poland

It was my first time flying, and my mother feared the plane would fall out of the sky. Then, there was the weather. We traveled at the start of spring when the temperature was still too cold by Cuban standards. In March, temperatures in Warsaw typically ranged between forty- and fifty degrees Fahrenheit, and I had no proper winter clothes. So, what did my mother do? She made me gloves from floor rags and wrapped plastic around them. She also gave me two sweaters she had purchased in the 1950s and suggested I wear several layers under them.

If before traveling to Warsaw, I didn't have a reason to feel attractive, now that I was going to be walking around Poland's capital wearing my mother's old sweaters—that were too big on me—and my ugly, ridiculous-looking gloves, there were plenty of reasons to feel that way.

My father had told me about Warsaw's troubled history. In 1944, German forces had destroyed from 80% to 90% of its buildings. It was thought that no other city worldwide suffered more significant losses. After the war, the rebuilding efforts brought the city back from the ashes. So, in 1973, when I walked on Warsaw's streets, watching the heavy traffic, children flying kites in city parks, and tall modern buildings nestled among historical ones—that somehow had stood the test of war and time—I couldn't help but to admire the resiliency of the Polish people.

We stayed at a small hotel and performed at a theater for the two weeks our engagement lasted. We had little money to spend, so during our free hours, we either stayed at the hotel or walked around the city, trying to stay within a reasonable distance and carefully documenting how to get back. The last thing we wanted was to get lost in Warsaw without speaking the language.

Although I had been sent to Warsaw to entertain dignitaries and high-ranking officials, I felt that the ability to see places beyond the confines of my tropical island had changed me. The world was grand and complex, and I was eager to discover it.

Just a year before, Fidel Castro, dressed in his olive-green uniform, had traveled from Budapest to Warsaw to meet with Polish Premier Pietr Jaroszewicz and Communist party chief Edward Gierek. So you might understand how I felt. Little me was visiting a place that the president of the island himself had recently visited.

In the 1970s, Cuba allowed only performers and government officials to travel abroad. Although I was no different than a pony sent to the circus to perform, I was glad that I caught a glimpse of a world that had been denied until then.

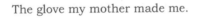

The glove my mother made me.

Chapter 15

The Proposal

After my job with *Los Llamas* ended, I had no other option but to become a soloist. Also, to supplement my income, I performed with groups that needed a pianist for only one or two engagements. I liked interacting with other band members but was thankful that being a soloist had brought Adam into my life. I felt so lucky to be with someone like him. Sometimes, he got me flowers he picked up from a garden. Other times, he brought me cookies or chocolates. I still loved chocolates!

When I was around Adam, I felt at ease and could be myself, but I could also feel strange sensations I had never felt before. Somehow, I could breathe better, and my days seemed brighter.

Unlike other technicians, Adam didn't live at the Hotel Sierra Maestra but at *El Reparto Flores* (Flores neighborhood) near *El Reparto Naútico*. Before 1959, only the wealthy lived in these affluent areas where the Havana Yacht Club and the Biltmore were located. After 1959, this zone had been designated for high-ranking officials and foreign visitors. These exclusive clubs were deliberately renamed La Concha, Siboney, and others and were converted to social clubs. Only those employees working for specific sectors of the economy had access to them. So, they were still exclusive but controlled by the government.

I wondered why Adam lived in the more affluent section of the city and not at the hotel with the other technicians, but it was difficult enough to communicate, so I didn't ask him why. I concluded he had a higher position.

Adam was a good kisser and a gentleman. He always rushed to open doors for me and made me feel like the only woman in the world. Occasionally, as I played the piano, we exchanged glances and smiled, but I tried to limit those interactions for fear of losing my job. However, every time he came to see me, I played his favorite song, "Bésame Mucho."

On weekends, Adam and I went to the Coppelia or the movie theater El Yara and held hands while walking around *El Vedado*.

One day, after my performance at the Sierra Maestra Hotel bar, we took a picture together to capture one of the happiest moments in my life.

As my relationship with Adam progressed, I invited him to a job function that my parents, Alfredo and Anita, planned to attend. It was like the celebration where my father introduced me to Celeste Mendoza, which was full of music and dancing. I was both excited and nervous about introducing him to my family.

That evening, when my mother saw Adam under the yellow glow of a garden lamp, she acted differently than I had expected. She smiled nervously and asked me to translate for her, but I explained that I still didn't speak his language. Frustrated, she yelled at him as if doing so would help

71

him understand her better. Despite the barriers, my parents and brother gave Adam approving glances. However, my mother confessed that she didn't like his long sideburns.

A few months after the celebration, Adam invited me to a restaurant near *El Malecón*, Havana's waterfront. He had an important matter to discuss. During our dinner, I kept asking him with hand movements, "What do you need to tell me?"

He held his palms up and moved them towards me several times, signaling me to wait. He then reached across the table for my hands and squeezed them softly as we smiled. God, he looked so handsome that evening.

As each of us was enjoying a delicious flan, he retrieved a small box from his pocket and gave it to me. His eyes lit up as I grabbed it and looked at it.

"What is it?" I asked.

"Open," he replied. He must have learned that word.

I opened it slowly, and my heart pounded heavily when I saw it.

It was a silver ring.

"Oh my God, Adam!" I said, covering my mouth with my hand in shock.

"You, me, marry?" he said.

I opened my eyes wide. With hand gestures, I asked him how. I lived in Cuba, and he was in Czechoslovakia. I knew his assignment was about to end, even though I had been trying to forget it. I wanted each moment I had with him to count.

"Come with me," he said in broken Spanish.

The Proposal

He wanted me to marry him and move with him to Czechoslovakia. I could never have imagined he would like me to accompany him.

"What about my family?" I asked.

He understood my question.

"We visit," he replied.

"I can't leave my parents! They are getting older and need me."

"I talked to them," he said slowly. "They said you move, okay."

"You went to speak to my parents?"

He nodded.

"Adam, I love you. I do. I don't know what I was thinking. I wanted to believe that your assignment would be renewed and that you could somehow stay in Cuba. It didn't occur to me that you would need to return one day."

He seemed confused.

"I would love nothing more than to marry you," I said, hoping he would understand me. "Let me talk to my parents," I added, talking with my hands.

There are critical crossroads in our lives, and I was facing one. I returned the ring to Adam and promised to talk to my parents. He didn't want to accept it back at first. I told him I would take it after speaking with my parents. I did that very same night.

"You should marry him and go," my mother said, but I read a different opinion in my father's eyes.

"Your mother is right," he said. I imagined how difficult it must have been to agree to let me go.

"I can never leave you," I said. "I love you both and could never live far away."

"We are going to die one day," my mother said. "You need to have a life."

"But not away from here where you, my brother, and my nephews are."

"Milagros," my mother added. "The day might come when you will regret this decision. Don't you love this man?"

"I do! You know I do, but I can't pay such a high price."

I spoke with Adam the day after my performance. In less than a week, he would be leaving Cuba. For years, I would second-guess myself and wonder what if. What if I had made a different decision? But he was destined to come into my life only to show me how beautiful love can be.

I kept the picture we took of us together among my most prized possessions. Over the months and years that followed, I wondered what had become of him. I imagined him married with three children and a good wife. I envisioned him living a happy life. I also wondered if I would ever love again, but like the poem *In Memoriam A.H.H.* by Alfred Lord Tennyson said, "Tis better to have loved and lost, than never to have loved at all."

Chapter 16

Carnaval

After Adam left, my life needed a new direction. By then, my grandmother Reimunda had died. My mother thought she had died of old age. True, she was old, but my father thought that sadness may have been a factor in her demise. In her last days, when I came to visit her at Aunt Angelita's house and found her sitting in a wheelchair, I could see grief in her eyes. On her better days, when dementia didn't take her back to her earlier years, she recognized me. Other times, she called me by the name of one of the daughters living in the United States.

My father told me that if dementia ever got a hold of him, he preferred to be dead. I wouldn't say I liked it when he spoke about death like that. I wanted to believe that he and my mother would live forever.

Wishing to remain positive, I concentrated on my two nephews, Alfredito and William. They were two precious children I loved like my own, with dark blond hair and brown eyes. When I played with them, I became another child. They loved the game of hide-and-seek and laughed as if they were being tickled.

I was so proud of them that I showed some of my patrons their pictures. They knew that life was difficult for people in Cuba, so sometimes they brought my nephews a toy or cookies.

By 1974, most of the women who were close to me when I was growing up were married and had children. Laura, Angelita's daughter, had three children, but her husband had left Cuba in 1968. He wanted to get his family out of Cuba once he saved money for his family's visas. Just as he was able to secure the visas, Fidel Castro stopped allowing people to leave Cuba, and my cousin and her husband remained separated with the uncertainty of reuniting again any time soon. Her sister, Berta, had married an engineer a few months after Aunt Angelita died. The couple had postponed having children, but after the policy changed, they decided they were stuck in Cuba. So, they were now trying to become parents.

I wanted a husband like my cousins, so I went out with a few men but kept comparing them to Adam. That magic we had together could not be duplicated.

Not happy with my current situation, I decided to do something drastic that would take me out of my comfort zone. That was when the idea of participating in Havana's annual carnival came to mind. I wanted to dance on one of the floats. Years earlier, my mother would not have supported this idea, but she must have realized I needed to do something. She even helped secure the forms I had to complete to make it happen.

My supportive and wise father thought it was a clever idea to tell me about the history of the

Carnaval. I enjoyed listening to his stories and seeing how his eyes grew smaller and his dimples more pronounced when he smiled.

Sitting on his favorite rocking chair in the living room, my father went back to the beginning of the celebrations.

The Havana *Carnaval* became a permanent feature of life and culture in 1937. It paraded through the *Paseo del Prado* street with contagious dances and choreographies that inspired spectators to move their bodies to the music. It was as if the music from popular groups like *Los Guaracheros de Regla* and *El Alacrán*, two of the most popular, possessed the people's bodies as they passed. Detailed and colorful floats illuminated the night while people drank and danced along their path. The dancers riding on the float—men and women— dressed in exotic attire, the women bearing tall head decorations that made them look like goddesses. That was how my father described them while my mother rolled her eyes.

In 1959, after Fidel Castro came to power, the month of the celebrations was changed from February and March to July. My father thought that the change had to do with an important date for the triumph of the Cuban revolution, Castro's and his revolutionaries' assault on the Moncada Barracks on July 26, 1953. I didn't care about such events. After all, the revolution had divided my family. I only cared about the celebrations and what they meant to me, an opportunity to make people smile.

I was excited when I was chosen to dance on the float belonging to the Department of Tourism

(Intur). As shy as I had been in my teenage years, I felt uncomfortable standing on the well-lit and colorful float, dancing and waving to the spectators. We used to practice at the social club *José Antonio Echevarria*. One day, Manolito, the son of a cook who worked at the Hotel Nacional where my father worked, saw me practicing and darted toward me.

"Milagros, what are you doing here?" he asked, as if in shock to see me.

"Practicing to dance at the carnival."

"Does your mother know that? Once she finds out, she's going to be furious."

"Yes, relax. My mother knows," I replied without stopping my rehearsal.

"You can't be serious. This is not the place for you. You're a nice young woman. When my parents hear about it, they won't believe it."

A dancer who was practicing next to me stopped dancing and placed her hands on her hips, "What are you saying that I'm a whore for dancing at the carnival?" she shouted at him.

"That's not what I'm saying. I'm just surprised to see my friend Milagros here. No need to get upset."

"Trust me, Manolito. Both my parents know, and there is nothing wrong with doing this. I'm still the same person."

And I meant every word. When I danced on the float, I didn't even take a break to avoid mingling with drunk men in the crowd who might cross the line. While on the float, I was untouchable and protected by the dancers around me.

By the time I joined the carnival, Aunt Angelita had already died. So, my mother had to make my outfit herself with whatever fabric she could find. My top almost looked like part of a bikini but much more conservative, with a black background and white ovals. I also wore a long white skirt tied in the front. As for my headpiece, I asked the other dancers to help me design it. My headpiece looked like something from another dimension, which made me laugh when my mother snapped my picture. I smiled not with the type of smile that suggested, "Look how pretty I am," but with one that said, "I cannot believe that I'm dancing on top of this float looking this ridiculous."

I thought that one day, among the crowd, I would see Adam again. I thought he would return to stay in Cuba and restart where we left off. I know it might sound naïve, but dreaming has a strange way of keeping us hopeful, and hope is the last thing one should lose.

And so, I danced at the carnival for six or seven years. That is until the quality of the floats began to decrease due to the lack of materials needed to maintain them.

Carnaval

Dancing on a float at the carnival – Havana 1972

Chapter 17

1979

By 1979, my father had retired and decided to trade our house in Mantilla for one close to the baseball stadium *Estadio Latinoamericano* in the *El Cerro* neighborhood in Havana. The stadium was so close to our house that a ball sometimes landed in our backyard when a player hit a home run.

My father's rationale for the move was two-fold: He would have easy access to baseball games and food. It may not be easy to understand this if you did not live in Cuba in 1979, so I will try to explain. The food we could buy through the *Tarjeta de Abastecimiento* (rationing card) kept dwindling. When it was time to buy our monthly quota, sometimes neither chicken nor beef came to the bodega assigned to us. On the other hand, chícharos (split peas) became abundant, but you can only eat them for so long before you start seeing them in your dreams.

In Cuba, unlike in other parts of the world, people could not go to a supermarket and buy what they wanted. Not back in 1979. The stadium, however, provided us with a gastronomic feast. A small restaurant there sold *pan con croquetas* (croquettes sandwiches), pizza, and *refrescos* (drinks).

And everyone at our house loved baseball. We were always on the side of the *Industriales* team. So, when we got bored, or it was too hot to be in the house, we all went to the stadium, bought a refreshing *malta* (malt) and pizza, and watched a game. Thankfully, we had some disposable income between my father's pension and the wages of all the working-age adults who lived in our house.

Back in 1979, the *Industriales* used to have excellent players, like Lázaro Valles, a fantastic pitcher, and Lázaro de la Torre, who everyone called *el látigo negro* (the black whip) because of the blackness of his skin and his talent as a hitter. There was also Lázaro Vargas. Strangely enough, there were a lot of Lázaros on that team.

When we moved, we had a dog named Bobby, so we took turns walking him around the stadium. I suspected that he was crazy, given the eight times he bit me. When he had epileptic seizures, he looked at me with so much sadness that I forgave him for his unprovoked attacks. I didn't like seeing animals suffer, and poor Bobby couldn't control his violent reactions.

One day, when my father was walking Bobby around the stadium, two German Shepherds caught Bobby's attention, and he ran toward them while the other dogs menacingly barked at him. My father tried to restrain Bobby, but the pulling in opposite directions between my father and Bobby caused the leash to snap. What happened next was difficult to witness. Bobby and the German Shepherds began to fight and tear each other apart. My father kept yelling his name and tried to get close, but he knew he was no match for three determined dogs. Ultimately, Bobby won the fight and returned home victorious with my father. After that, people in the neighborhood began to call him "Bobby, the Champion."

With Bobby by our side, we could leave our house open all day because we were confident no one would dare come in.

There was so much more that happened in 1979. In Cuba, young people danced to disco music at underground house parties. However, that year's most prominent news was Castro's opening of the island to expatriates after eleven years. You might remember that Laura, Angelita's daughter, had three children. Her husband left Cuba in 1968, and after Fidel Castro stopped allowing people to leave Cuba, Laura and her children remained separated from Rio, Laura's husband. Now, he could return through trips called *Viajes de la Comunidad* (trips of the community).

Rio, in his effort to surprise Laura and the children, almost killed her! When her oldest daughter, Tania, who was fourteen, opened the door and realized who the stranger was, she alerted her mother that someone was there to see her. Laura was watching television and didn't want to be bothered at first. Upon Tania's insistence, she turned around, screamed Rio's name, and fainted. Imagine what happened later. The house was filled with curious neighbors wanting to know everything about life in the United States.

From then on, thousands of people living comfortably in Miami and other U.S. cities came to Cuba, which meant more work for me. I asked my father, "Papi, do you think this opening will help Fidel Castro?"

He replied, "I am glad that families can now see each other, but this will also lift the veil off the people's eyes when they see that people who left as *gusanos* (worms) return like butterflies." Worms is the derogatory term Castro used for the people who had left Cuba.

Whenever someone from abroad visited a family member, it was as if a being from another planet had arrived. They dressed better than the locals and smelled of expensive colognes. They looked happier than most people on the island and ate better than we did in Cuba.

This event would unchain a series of outcomes that would impact my life in ways I never imagined.

Chapter 18

Mother's Words to Lenin

At the end of the 1970s, *Habana Tours* began to grant applications to allow a select group of citizens to travel. Only those well-connected with the Communist Party had access to these applications. But I wasn't involved in the party. Like my father, I didn't care about politics, only about creating music. However, I made many friends during my multiple performances.

A saying in Cuba is that those with friends own a factory (*quien tiene amigos tiene un central*). So, through one of the connections I made while playing the piano, someone with close ties to the government, I was able to obtain two travel applications, one for my mother and one for me. When I held those applications, I realized how lucky I was to have them. I couldn't wait to travel again, but this time, I wanted to do so as a tourist, not a worker.

I had enjoyed my first *two* trips out of Cuba so much that I wanted my mother to have the same experiences I did. I say two trips because after going to Warsaw, our band had another engagement in the Soviet Union.

I felt terrible that I was only able to secure two applications. However, my father said that he had already traveled extensively when he lived in Spain. Also, he thought my mother and I deserved to have such experiences. "Traveling is the best education," he said.

Traveling was one way my piano career opened paths that otherwise would not have been available. Not only could we travel, but the trips were heavily discounted.

I was so excited when my mother and I sat together in an airplane for the first time. I couldn't wait to show her the fabulous world I had seen. But I knew the people who accompanied us on this trip—and my mother and I—were part of a privileged few. Throughout this trip, I kept reminding myself that I would never have been on that plane if my parents had not purchased me a piano as a child. I would have been like everyone else, stuck in Cuba for the rest of my natural life and going to bed hungry most days.

This trip would take us to the Soviet Union, Germany's Socialist Republic, Poland, Hungary, Romania, Bulgaria, and Czechoslovakia. And I know what you must think when reading the last name on the list. The notion that I might see Adam during our visit to Czechoslovakia or other countries crossed my mind and invigorated me. I thought that these doors had opened for me because we were destined to cross paths again.

It was the second half of May, a perfect time to visit these countries that would have been unbearable for us in the wintertime.

As part of the Cuban delegation, our excursions were prearranged. Each of us received the equivalent of $5 per day, a fortune in those days, which allowed us to purchase shoes and clothes for ourselves, my brother, father, and nephews.

I will never forget watching my mother walking in Gorky Park, a place of culture and leisure off the banks of the Moskva River. We had never seen a park as beautiful as that one, with well-kept, lush greenery and flowers in full bloom. We watched people sitting at a café by the river, others enjoying the explosion of colors of the Golitsynsky Garden, and families walking on crowded promenades. We also admired the 17th-century, Italian-inspired estates where noble families once lived.

On the second day, we experienced the magnificence of the Kremlin, a 15th-century complex composed of five palaces once home to the Tsar family. This was the heart of the Soviet government, the center of power. Then, our guide took us to Red Square to visit the tomb of Vladimir Lenin, leader of the Bolshevik Party and the Soviet Union until he died in 1924. The massive mausoleum and solemn, almost haunting, music inside it impressed me, but even more so, how my mother stood by Lenin's tomb, lost in thought. Later, back at the hotel—when none of the people in our tour group were around—I asked her why she had stood there for so long.

"I was talking to him," she said.

"About what?"

"You want me to tell you?"

"Yes. What would you have to tell him?"

"I told him, 'It is all your fault, son-of-a-bitch. Because of your ideals, families in Cuba are separated. Because of you, my people go hungry. You and people like you brought a horrible plague into the world. I hope you rot in Hell.' That's what I told him."

I was shocked. I knew I wasn't savvy about the world around me. I also would have never established the connection between Lenin and what was happening in Cuba because I was too young when Castro came to power. I became a teenager under Castro's government. So I could only say, "Why didn't you tell me?"

"Why?"

"So I could tell him the same thing."

In all the years I had lived with my mother, she had never spoken about her feelings about the revolution and communism. I could not believe that a trip to the Soviet Union would unearth those feelings. Once it did, I felt I could understand her outbursts better. I also realized she was wiser than I thought.

The next day, I saw things differently as we admired the buildings and fountains surrounding the neoclassical Bolshoi Theater—home to the world-renowned Bolshoi ballet and opera company. I also looked at the people more closely and wondered if they were going to bed hungry, like many people in Cuba. I wondered if they were happy. The answer to my question would reveal itself several years later.

Me in Moscow

Chapter 19

Looking for Adam

After a few days in Moscow, some people in my group complained about the food. They wanted bean soup, any bean—black, white, red, or garbanzo. By then, I had learned to speak a few Russian words, so my group used me as the official translator. I guess I didn't do a good job translating because the following day, for breakfast, the servers showed up with cups containing a pale liquid with white beans in them. They also brought scrambled eggs and potatoes.

"What's that?" I asked, pointing at the pale liquid.

"White bean soup, like you requested."

"For breakfast?" one of the men in our group asked.

The chubby, red-faced woman shrugged.

"Thank you," I said, hoping she would walk away.

After she left, a man said, "Who in their right mind would have bean soup for breakfast?" Then, after tasting it, he added, "Who taught them how to make white bean soup? This is horrible!"

So much for my translation skills; we had no choice but to eat what the Soviets ate. Soon, we grew tired of *rassolnik*, a soup containing pickled cucumbers, *shchi*, cabbage soup, and borscht.

***

The second city we visited in the Soviet Union, Leningrad (which later became St. Petersburg), was far less intimidating and approachable. I felt that I could breathe better there. Even the people seemed friendlier. The city was home to the spectacular Hermitage Museum, one of the largest in the world. Leningrad was regal and grand. We admired the opulent churches and palaces and the areas surrounding the canals. Nevsky Avenue was perfect for people-watching and an ideal place to search for Adam. But again, no luck.

While in Budapest, Hungary's capital, we marveled at the Széchenyi Chain Bridge, rising in all its splendor over the Danube River, and the iconic and massive Parliament Building, with its gothic and baroque styles, standing on the banks of the river. I knew nothing about architectural styles until the tour guide explained them to me. This made me think about my father's words about how traveling could be the best education I would ever have.

I looked for Adam in every city and grew disappointed when I didn't see him.

I thought I might find him at our last stop, Prague, Czechoslovakia's capital. He had told me he lived there, but I didn't know where exactly.

As we walked through Old Town, I searched for him among the faces in the crowd. If we only had more time. But Prague was a big city with over

900,000 people back then. When I saw the size of this place, I realized I would never find him.

Below: Hungarian Parliament Building – Budapest

Chapter 20

1980

Havana seemed tense in the days before the occurrence of an event that would change life for thousands of people in Cuba. When the news finally spread throughout the city, my father felt validated.

"What did I tell you, Juana?"

"Yes, you said it," my mother replied, rolling her eyes. "You always know everything."

They were referring to the bus that went through the gates of the Peruvian Embassy in Havana carrying a group of people seeking political asylum.

Obtaining details about what happened was complicated, given that the government controlled the media. All I knew was that Castro unexpectedly removed Cuban police from the entrance to the embassy, and in little time, over 5,000 people flooded its grounds.

"People are tired of waiting for things to change," my father said.

"It makes sense. The rations keep getting smaller, the blackouts..." my mother replied. "And the government opened those new stores, the *diplo-tiendas*, full of groceries we have not seen since the early 1960s that only the tourists can access. What did you think would happen? It doesn't take a genius to figure it out."

It surprised me that my mother had become more vocal since our trip, especially in front of me, but I was twenty-nine already, no longer the child she wanted to protect.

A few days after the incident at the embassy, Castro announced that those who had relatives in the United States could come for them through the Port of Mariel. My mother didn't realize then that this measure would impact her family, not until May 2, 1980, when Berta, Aunt Angelita's youngest daughter, visited us. She told us that Rio, Laura's husband, had come for Laura and their three children. They had left Cuba through the Port of Mariel. Twelve years had passed since Rio left, so the children were then fifteen, thirteen, and eleven. The oldest two were the same age as my nephews Alfredito and William.

Only a month after the incursion into the embassy, our family had lost four more members to exile.

Laura was my mother's dearest niece. Not that she didn't care for Berta, but she and Berta were never close. The news also affected my brother Alfredo, who viewed Laura like a sister. He was closer to her than he had ever been to me.

"I am also trying to leave Cuba with my family," Berta said.

My mother sat across from Berta and fanned herself with a piece of cardboard.

"Soon, there won't be anyone left," my mother said pensively. "I'm glad that your grandmother

Reimunda is dead. Otherwise, it would have killed her to witness what happened to her family."

"You know we don't have a choice," Berta said. "You know what's happening here to people like us. Many are being dragged out of their houses and beaten by government thugs."

"I know. I understand why you're leaving. And you have two young daughters to worry about. Don't you think it upsets me when I hear that teenagers are selling their bodies for a pair of jeans? We are fortunate that Milagros became a pianist when she did. It's no secret that she has more opportunities than most on this island."

"Why don't you leave?" Berta asked, lowering her tone after noticing the windows were open. "You have an established family in Miami. They might be willing to come for you."

My mother inhaled deeply. She then glanced at a picture of Abuela Reimunda on the wall.

"My mother never wanted her children to become immigrants. Life had been so difficult for her when she came to Cuba."

"But things are different in the United States."

"Time has passed us by. We are too old to start all over," my mother replied. Then, after a short silence, she added, "Besides, I deserve to feel the aftermath. Like a fool, I believed in the revolution at first. I thought it might help the people."

"Don't be so hard on yourself. Many people did what you did. And what about Milagros? Why can't she leave?" Berta asked, turning her head toward me.

"I'm not leaving my parents," I said. "They are getting old, and they need me."

My mother shook her head.

"I tried to convince her to leave when she met that nice Czechoslovakian engineer," she said. "She refused. She's a hardhead like me. As for me, don't forget that I have two grandchildren and my son Alfredo. Milagros adores her nephews. Our roots here are too deep."

I was saddened to see my mother, not like the lioness she was when I was growing up, but like someone who felt defeated.

Love, loss, and disappointments tested her resilience, slowly eroding the vibrant person she once was. And this was only the beginning.

Chapter 21

My Father

My father always had an enviable memory. Then, gradually, he started having problems remembering things. A visit to the doctor confirmed my worst fears.

I told you earlier that I am a half-glass-full person. I focus on the positive. So, I kept telling myself that the doctors were wrong and that my father would get better. But his cognitive abilities kept deteriorating. At the time, I was working at the Tritón Hotel in the Playa Municipality by the beach. It was the first hotel to be built in Havana after 1959. Now that more people from the United States were visiting the island, my tips kept growing, and many were in dollars, a currency that could be used at the *diplotiendas*. I was happy that, through my connections, I could buy food at these stores and bring it home to my parents. I hoped that the improved diet would help my father get better.

It isn't easy to see a parent wither away, like a fallen leaf that slowly turns brown and shrivels.

In 1983, we moved from our place by the stadium to Centro Habana. Watching baseball games was no longer fun when my father couldn't enjoy them. A more central location near hotels and restaurants where I could work made more sense. After we moved, Mamá didn't want to leave my father's side and hardly ate. She became so thin during his final days that we feared for her well-being.

My father went with God peacefully on a sunny Saturday afternoon in 1988, with the family gathered around him and my mother and me holding his hands. Alfredo, his wife Anita, and their two adult sons, now in their twenties, were there. Although we knew his suffering had ended when he took his last breath, we couldn't avoid the tears that rolled down our cheeks. I embraced my tearful mother and held her while Alfredo and I exchanged glances. Then, my mother sought refuge in her grandsons' arms. Alfredo, with eyes full of emotion, looked at me awkwardly. I knew what he needed, so I opened my arms, and we embraced. This time, he wasn't faking his feelings towards me. I could sense it. We were both hurting and knew we could only overcome the pain by supporting each other.

Over the months that followed my father's death, I stopped being who I was. It was as if half of myself had been taken away. I had been my father's little girl, the child he felt he needed to protect, and now my protector was gone. It was the first time I had experienced such a significant loss. Yes, Abuela Reimunda and Aunt Angelita had died, but I didn't see them every day. Losing a parent is different. It changes us. It transforms us into a different person, an introspective one who looks at the world through a new lens. We begin to fear that it won't be long before the remaining parent leaves us, too, and that we will one day follow. Losing a parent helps us come face to face with our inevitable demise.

I didn't want to look at the world this way.

I was given three days to mourn my father's death, but it wasn't enough. So, when I returned to the hotel to play for the tourists, I felt like one of my legs was missing. My music became more melancholic, and my tips grew smaller. People didn't want to feel my sorrow. They came to the hotel to escape their problems and be entertained. They sought relaxation.

So, I had to become the old me again because my family's survival depended on it.

The show had to go on.

My parents – 1942

Chapter 22

Celeste Mendoza

I never thought I would see Celeste Mendoza, the singer who inspired me to become a performer, again. However, life has a strange way of reconnecting us with our past. That afternoon, around 1989, about a year after losing my father, I played the piano at the elegant restaurant La Torre on the top floor of the FOCSA Building. Centrally situated in El Vedado near the interception of streets M and N, this building was Cuba's tallest. As I played while surrounded by the sound of plates and utensils and the quiet conversations around me, I felt as if I was on top of the world.

During my performance, a few customers came over to leave a peso or two in my jar. Some people deposited a dollar or other currency in my jar that I couldn't use. Some stood by me for a few moments and nodded in approval.

By now, I no longer feared being on stage. Quite the opposite; when playing at restaurants, I didn't have the blinding spotlight of a stage on me, which allowed me to glance at the crowd. I enjoyed doing so occasionally.

On this sunny afternoon, as I looked around the room, only a few meters away, I noticed a familiar face. I couldn't believe it. Occasionally, she would turn in my direction, seeming to enjoy what I was playing. I could tell by the way she moved her body and smiled.

When my performance ended, I shyly approached her.

"Are you Celeste Mendoza?" I asked, afraid I could have confused her with someone else.

"Yes, I am," she said.

"I know you get to meet many people in your profession as one of the best singers in Cuba. So, I'm sure you don't remember me. My father Angelito worked at the Hotel Nacional, and one day, he introduced me to you."

I explained what happened and how that encounter had changed my life. Despite the years, Celeste still looked like a star. She smelled of expensive perfume and dressed elegantly, her hair combed back neatly and gathered in a fancy bun. Her smile brightened the room as she spoke.

"I saw you and wanted to thank you," I said. "Few times do we get to thank those who inspire us. You changed my life."

Her eyes glistened.

"I remember your dad," she said. "Good man. How is he doing?"

"He passed away last year," I replied.

"I'm so sorry. But I am glad he introduced me to you, and I am even happier that my words impacted you. I wish I had met you sooner. I would have loved to perform on stage with you. You are exceptionally talented."

"You mean it?"

"Absolutely. You should be proud of yourself. And I am sure your father looks at you from above and smiles each time you play the piano."

That was the last time I saw Celeste. I read that she died nine years later, on November 22, 1998. Her death was reported in The New York Times, where they called her The Queen of Guaguancó (street rumba). The cause of death wasn't disclosed, but years later, people would rumor that she had died of respiratory failure after years of heavy drinking.

She died alone, and her body was discovered days after her death. When I heard the news, I wondered if I, too, would die alone, if anyone would ever write about me in New York newspapers. Then, I came to my senses. Of course not.

Who would ever write about a lonely pianist who played at restaurants and bars?

Chapter 23

The Russians

In the late 1980s, I played the piano at the Amistad Hotel, later known as The Koli Hotel, which housed Soviet military advisors and their families. One day, a young, fair-skinned, blue-eyed couple with their two little boys approached me and stood by the piano to watch me play. I momentarily lifted my eyes from the keys to acknowledge them with a slight nod and a smile. To my dismay, after I finished playing my first song, the female spoke to me in perfect Spanish.

"You play beautifully," she said. "I could listen to you forever." I thanked her.

"Do you have a special request?" I asked her.

"Oh, I don't know the titles of songs, but I'm sure anything you pick is fine. You have a way of getting into people's hearts."

"You are looking at me with kind eyes. I'm nothing special."

"See? I didn't have to know how humble you were. I could see it in your eyes. You transport yourself and others around you to an extraordinary place when you play. And it's as if you don't realize you're doing it, as if you don't know just how talented you are."

The Russians

My face reddened. I had received many compliments before, but none as direct—not since I was dating Adam. I was once again thinking about him. Many years had passed since I last saw him, and I still couldn't keep him off my mind. I hoped to see him again one day. I was so pathetic that I kept his picture hidden, for God's sake. But I didn't want anyone to know how I felt about him. It was my secret.

The young couple standing by the piano brought memories of Adam and me together. They looked as happy as we were.

Natasha and Vladimir introduced themselves and their children, and this was the beginning of a close friendship. During the month that they stayed at the *Amistad Hotel*, they talked to me about their lives. Natasha worked for a Russian airline that flew in and out of Cuba, and Vladimir was the assistant to Raul Castro's Soviet military advisor. She seemed interested in learning about the economic conditions on the island, and once I told her, she wanted to help my family.

Soviet military advisors and their families had access to a warehouse containing all the provisions unavailable to Cubans on the island. So, Natasha would bring me canned goods from this special store. She and her family even visited our house by car. Later, after the family had moved to a beautiful house near the hotel, I, too, visited them. During one of my visits to Natasha, she gave me a few cans of Russian meat (*Tushonka*), and I brought them home.

My mother had always avoided Russian canned meat because people rumored it was made of bear, but later, I learned it was beef or pork. The first time I opened a can, I noticed a mixture of lard, jelly, and chunky meat. I tasted it. It wasn't bad, but my mother added spices to the meat and cooked it her way, making it taste even better.

As the weeks passed, Natasha and I kept getting closer. One day, when I visited her, she asked me, "So, do you have any boyfriends?"

She was in the ample kitchen, making beef stroganoff as we spoke.

"I've had a few, but none that are memorable."

She stopped what she was doing and turned toward me.

"Oh, come on," she said. "There must have been someone special."

I remained silent and looked down. I sensed her looking at me.

"I knew it!" she said as if she had been able to read my thoughts. "Who was he?"

I shrugged. "It's silly to talk about it. It has been such a long time since I saw him."

I was so transparent that I had no choice but to tell her my secret. She listened attentively.

"That is so romantic," she said. "So sad you let him go, but I understand you didn't want to leave your family. It has been so difficult for me to be separated from my family in the Soviet Union."

"I can imagine," I said.

Now that Natasha knew my secret, I felt even closer to her. It was like having a sister, as ridiculous as that sounded.

One day, in 1991, I was visiting Natasha when Vladimir arrived unexpectedly. She and I

The Russians

were sitting on the sofa and rose to greet him. He wore a military uniform and had a worried look on his reddened face. Violently, he retrieved his wallet, searched for something, and threw a card across the floor.

"It's all over!" he shouted in Spanish. "Everything has gone to hell!"

I had never seen this mild-mannered young man so upset.

She placed her hand on her chest. I felt like an intruder, but I wanted to know what was happening.

"Communism has fallen in the Soviet Union. It failed!" he said. I opened my eyes wide. My questions from my trips to the Soviet Union had been answered. Now, I knew that the people I had seen walking on the promenades in Moscow and Leningrad were unhappy.

I couldn't tell Vladimir what I was thinking, but I spoke to him in my mind, "Are you surprised?"

They had been nice to me, so I felt terrible for him. He looked so desperate and lost.

"But I don't understand. Just like that?" Natasha asked, grabbing his hands. The children had stopped playing in their room and joined us.

"Please go back to your room," Natasha said. "Your mom and dad have something serious to discuss."

The children obeyed. After they were gone, I said, "I should go. If there is anything I can do, please let me know."

I hugged Natasha and left.

The Russians

I knew little about the factors that caused communism to fail and wondered if Cuba would follow.

Later, I learned that since taking power in 1985, Russian President Mikhail Gorbachev had instituted new policies to revitalize the Communist Party: *glasnost* (openness) and *perestroika* (restructuring). But instead of fixing the system, the state lost media control, which opened the floodgates to criticism about the shortages and mismanagement of fiscal affairs.

Within a few months after the fall of communism in the countries of the European Eastern Bloc, the hotel where I worked became a ghost town as Russians returned home. Vladimir was the first one to leave. Natasha was supposed to follow shortly after, but there was so much red tape and confusion around this time. Like Natasha and her boys, who were stuck in Cuba, Mayda, one of my cousins studying in Russia, was trapped there, and it took her weeks to return to Cuba.

"There was so much confusion when communism fell," Mayda told me. "No one knew what to do or when we would be able to come home."

That same confusion existed in Cuba. A few weeks after Vladimir left, Natasha and her boys were removed from the lovely house where they lived and placed in a hotel for low-level Russians, a place so inadequate that people called it the flea market (*pulguero*).

I visited her there, and she told me the Cuban government was hardly feeding her family. They were going hungry.

"I can't believe they would treat us like this after my country did so much for the Cubans," she told me. I shared this with my mother, who had lost all faith in the revolution by then.

"If these people have killed their own, if they don't feed us and treat us like second-class citizens in our own country, what can a foreigner, who is no longer deemed to be useful, expect? The Russians exceeded their period of expiration. And now, they will be discarded like garbage."

Life was becoming more difficult for us, but I couldn't turn my back on someone who once helped my family. So, one day, I brought Natasha and her children an omelet. That was all I could do for her.

Natasha left Cuba a few days later, and I never saw her again.

Chapter 24

Special Period

I wished my father had been alive to help explain why, after communism fell in the Soviet Union and Eastern Europe in 1991, Cuba went into an economic meltdown. I liked the way he explained things to me. Luckily, Alfredo had taken my father's role of reducing complex issues to simple explanations. He told me that 80% of Cuba's imports and exports had disappeared overnight. Imagine if that happened in your country.

During what became known as "The Special Period in Time of Peace," there was hardly any fuel for the few cars on the road, so people had to rely on alternative transportation. The government then ordered 1.2 million bicycles from China and began to redirect some factories to bicycle production. Accidents skyrocketed with so many bicycles on the roads, especially at night. But bicycles could only take bicyclists so far. Therefore, some buses were retrofitted to carry bikes and riders closer to their destinations. During this period, a mode of transport called *camellos* surfaced, an eighteen-wheeler bus that had two humps, like a camel's back, and could transport hundreds of standing passengers.

Food insecurity and rolling blackouts prevailed during this period. So, we often spent the last few hours of our day talking under the yellow glow of a Chinese kerosene lamp. When it was too hot to be inside, we sat on the balcony and watched the dark city below. Even under an envelope of darkness, I found Havana appealing and intriguing, which could explain why those who left this island never forgot about this place.

From my balcony, I could hear my neighbors' voices. "Pedrito, do we have more kerosene?" "No, Mami, it ran out." "Anita, where is the dog? Did you leave the door open?" "It is too hot inside, Mami! I'm melting!"

If rations had already diminished before the Special Period, soon even more drastic cuts from those low levels occurred. Power outages sometimes lasted six hours or more. People often went to bed hungry, consuming significantly less than 2,000 calories daily. Many of my friends had lost a fifth of their weight or more. While Castro called this period of severe food shortages the "Special Period," some called it the "Great Famine."

Food and electricity were not the only victims. Hospitals turned into veritable wastelands due to the lack of maintenance and basic supplies. Due to the state of despair, hospital workers became so discouraged by their hunger and lack of adequate supplies to do their jobs that they nearly stopped caring.

Around 1992, the government gave those they deemed "good revolutionaries" a pizza coupon, entitling them to purchase one personal pizza. I secured a couple for my mother and me. By this

110

time, Alfredo and his family did not live with us; they had moved to his mother-in-law's house.

On this humid day, we arrived at the pizza line before the sun had risen on the horizon when the grass still showed the shine of the morning dew. By then, the line was already four blocks long.

"Is this the line for the pizza?" I asked the young woman before me to ensure I was in the right place.

She nodded and smiled.

We took our place at the end of the line. Then, I counted the water bottles in my bag and wondered if they would be enough.

I paid closer attention to the couple in front of us. The young woman wore tiny shorts, and the man who accompanied her was shirtless and had long hair. That raised my mother's curiosity.

"Do both of you have coupons?" my mother asked. I figured she needed to do something to kill time.

"My girlfriend has one," he said. "But do I look like someone who would have a pizza coupon?"

My mother shook her head and sneered.

"You don't," she said.

The man laughed. "It's all about the people you know. Everything is for sale. That's why I have a coupon."

The young woman hit him in his rib with her elbow.

"Please don't pay attention to my boyfriend," the woman said. "He did earn his coupon."

"But I didn't!" he protested. "Besides, why are you hitting me, Elsa? I didn't do anything wrong?"

Elsa opened her eyes wide, and I understood perfectly what was happening.

After standing in line for two hours, we had only moved two blocks. Two more hours to go, I thought. To protect herself from the sun, my mother sat under the roof of the corner bodega. She looked so tired.

"If someone had told me after the revolution's triumph that I would be standing in line for hours to eat a piece of bread with some tomato sauce, I would have said they were crazy," she said, wiping the sweat off her forehead.

She remained silent for a moment before continuing. "And you know what the most frustrating thing is, I helped them! I'm part of the problem!"

"You can't blame yourself," I replied. "I know your heart was in the right place."

"I feel like such a fool."

Her eyes filled with tears.

"And your father told me. He knew where this country was headed. He predicted that one day I would regret helping them."

"Mamá, you shouldn't speak like that here," I said, afraid someone could overhear her and report her.

"I'm tired," she said. "I'm tired of staying quiet."

"You'll see," I said. "Soon, you will eat a tasty pizza and forget about all this."

She remained quiet. As the line moved, she grew pale with exhaustion. She had aged so much since my father's death and now had deep grooves under her cheekbones and on her forehead.

"Almost there, Mamá," I kept reassuring her.

As time passed, restlessness and frustration grew. At the end of our block, two people in line started a fistfight.

"Hunger is turning us into monsters," my mother said.

"There are always troublemakers everywhere, Mami," I replied.

After another two hours, we were closer to the front of the line. I could smell the cheese and freshly baked bread, and our stomachs growled.

"Almost there," I said again, rubbing my hands together.

We were about to enter the pizza place. A couple more people and our wait would be over. I fanned my mother with cardboard to help her cool down.

"Worry about yourself," she said, depleted of energy.

Moments later, a heavy, red-faced man wearing a white shirt and shorts exited the establishment.

"Please gather around," he said to the crowd. "I have an announcement to make."

My mother and I exchanged glances.

"What's going on?" people around us shouted.

He waited for people to be quiet.

Special Period

"I am deeply sorry to announce that there is no more pizza today. We just ran out of flour," he said.

"What do you mean there's no more pizza? We have been in line for four hours!" I shouted.

I glanced at my mother. She had brought her hand to her chest and looked very pale. Then, she let out a scream that paralyzed those around her. She then stumbled to the ground as I tried to grab her before her body hit the paved street. But I wasn't strong enough. Drenched in sweat, I hovered over her.

"What's wrong, Mamá?" I asked, gently slapping her cheeks.

She had fallen on her side, but now she lay flat, her eyes directed towards the sunny, blue sky. It was as if she could not hear me. All she could do was scream while the people around us watched. "Angelito, take me with you!" she cried. She closed her eyes while her tears streamed down the pavement.

I sat on the floor and poured some water over her face.

"Mami, please," I said. "Get up. I'll try to find a way to bring more food home so you don't have to stand in line for hours again. Mami, please."

This was a turning point for my mother. She was never the same. Like my father, she withered away until her heart gave out in 1993. She was done fighting.

By 1994, over 34,000 people left Cuba on makeshift rafts. They preferred to risk dying at sea than to live under the horrific existing conditions of the time. In August, thousands of people in Havana took to the streets near *El Malecón* (Havana's waterfront) to protest the economic conditions and lack of freedom. This protest was called *El Maleconazo*.

Now that my parents were gone, I still needed to fight for my brother and nephews.

I could not, would not, let them go hungry.

Chapter 25

Moving On

I played the piano at *El Patio Restaurant* (near *Plaza de la Catedral*), the *Moscú Restaurant* (until it burned down), and many other restaurants in Havana. Sometimes, I walked up to thirty blocks to and from work. Other times, I rode my bicycle. If I was assigned to work by the beach, I had no option but to take public transportation but left hours before to ensure I arrived on time.

I worked hard, always looking for places to earn a living, always taking advantage of all my connections. Through friends, I found a job at a social circle assigned to members of the Ministry of the Interior (MINIT)—*Círculo Cristino Naranjo*. There, I only worked Saturdays and Sundays from noon to 6 p.m. and had lunch at the cafeteria assigned to workers. My employers allowed me to buy food for two people. I would purchase meats and other foods at a meager price, available only to members of the Armed Forces and the Ministry of the Interior.

While buying the meals I would take home, I met Regla, the cafeteria manager. She would greet me joyfully when she saw me, her white teeth contrasting against her chocolate skin.

"So, how's your family, Milagros," she would ask me.

We exchanged a few pleasantries, and she would show me pictures of her granddaughter, her pride and joy. These friendly encounters eventually led to an extra piece of chicken or more rice to take home.

It had been challenging to obtain a job at the MINIT. I was subjected to a rigorous background check to ensure they could trust me. I understood how fortunate I was to work there. So, during the years I played the piano at this social circle, every weekend, I went home with enough food to last a week. That was, with careful planning. For example, if I brought home chicken, I would never throw away the bones. I used them to make chicken soup. Sometimes, instead of eating the chicken, I would make croquettes.

The underground economy flourished during this period, and I had money from tips. Buying goods on the black market allowed us to fill the gap.

People in Cuba said that necessity was the mother of invention. Necessity taught us to divide a meal for two people into multiple servings for multiple days.

Chapter 26

A Growing Family

By 1998, I was forty-seven and still unmarried. I had several boyfriends through the years, but none compared to Adam. I often thought about him and wondered if I would recognize him if I ever saw him again. By now, he probably had grown children and lived a happy life.

Based on Cuban standards, I had become an old maid. Luckily, by then, my nephew William had an eight-year-old daughter, beautiful and intelligent like her parents. His marriage didn't last long, but he and his wife remained friends. So, little Cecilia spent some weekends with William and me. I loved that little girl.

Alfredito, William's brother, was married but had no children. All the years he spent listening to me playing the piano must have rubbed off on him because he became the director of a dancers' group. I never knew him to be a dancer, but anything was possible in Cuba with the right connections.

One of Angelita's daughters, Laura, already had grandchildren. She lived in Tampa, Florida, with her growing family. She and her husband owned a small glass company they created after Rio's back was injured at a job, and he received a

$10,000 workers' compensation check. His back was never the same, but with the small business behind their house, he would work as many hours as possible, rest a little, and continue working.

Laura's sister Berta lived with her husband and two daughters in West Palm Beach, Florida. The remaining cousins and their families lived in Miami.

As united as the family had been in Cuba, in the United States, these connections were lost with time. During one of my conversations with Laura over the telephone, I asked her about this.

"Doesn't it bother you that the family is so spread apart and that your cousins and their families live their lives without caring whether you live or die?"

"Happiness is never complete," she told me. "It is a price I am willing to pay to live in freedom. All my sacrifices were worth it. The twelve years I spent away from Rio were an adequate price to pay for my children's future. My cousins are too busy worrying about their children's future. It is only normal."

Her words made me think about my grandmother Reimunda and her fears about leaving Cuba.

Could she have been wrong?

Chapter 27

1997

Alfredo never told me about Alfredito's plans, and I resented it. I had treated Alfredo's sons, William and Alfredito, like my own, so don't you think I deserved the courtesy of a goodbye?

I knew that Alfredito had gone to Veracruz, Mexico, as the director of a group of dancers. His mother, Anita, and wife, Melisa, accompanied him on this trip. Although Melisa performed as one of the dancers, she never took formal dancing lessons. She learned the choreography from the other dancers to be able to leave the country as part of the group. Anita was Alfredito's assistant. As you might suspect, Cubans are highly creative and resourceful, and Alfredito was proof of that ingenuity.

I didn't learn about the following events until much later.

Alfredito and his group had traveled to Mexico through the same arrangements that allowed me to travel all over South America and on my first two trips to Russia and Poland. We both were part of "one-sided" cultural exchanges. After the dance agreement in Veracruz ended, Alfredito told each dancer they could do whatever they wished. Alfredito, Melisa, and Anita then went to the embassy in Mexico to ask for political asylum.

"You must return to Cuba first and then request it from there," the official told them.

But Alfredito did not want to return. He knew what would happen once they did. They would never be able to leave Cuba again.

Alfredito, his wife, and his mother were only left with one choice: to pay a coyote in Mexico to take them to the United States. That took several days and all their savings. After they crossed the Rio Grande, the U.S. border police captured them and brought them to jail.

As you recall, Laura, Angelita's daughter, and her three children have lived in the United States since 1980 after reuniting with Rio, Laura's husband. So, Alfredito called Laura to ask her for help. To remain in the United States, Alfredito, Anita, and Melisa needed a sponsor and a few thousand dollars.

Laura was a unique woman. She could never say no to someone in need, even less to family. Her decision to help caused tension between Laura and Rio.

"I don't want anyone in our house. I'm too old for that. I need peace," Rio said.

"They are my family and in need," she replied. "We will gather the money they need and give them a place to stay until they receive their work permits."

"You will be the death of me, Laura!" Rio assured her. "Weren't the twelve years we spent apart enough of a sacrifice?"

But she thought he was bluffing.

Between Laura, her three adult children, and her sister Berta, they gathered the money Alfredito needed. Rio was so angry about Laura's defiance that a few days after she sent Alfredito the money, he had a stroke.

By the time Alfredito, Anita, and Melisa were released from jail and placed on a bus to Tampa, Florida, where Laura lived, Rio was already in a wheelchair and unable to speak.

Alfredito, Anita, and Melisa lived with Laura and Rio for months until they obtained job permits.

Rio died a year later from another stroke. He was only sixty.

I didn't find out about Alfredito's ordeal until he arrived at Laura's house, and he called me to explain that he was not returning to Cuba.

"How could you do this?" I asked him. "This is the place where you were born. He who doesn't love the land where he's born doesn't love anyone."

"I love Cuba," he replied. "But I don't love what it has become. I'm sorry, Tía Milagros. I had no choice. After I settle down, I'll send for you if you want."

"Why is it so difficult to understand that this is my home? This is where my parents are buried. I'm not going anywhere!"

And just like that, I lost another part of me. But I couldn't let sadness consume me. We were still in the Special Period, so I had to fight for my brother Alfredo and nephew William, who lived with me, and for my young niece.

They were worth fighting for.

1997

So, I returned to work the next day, sat behind a piano, and played as if nothing was wrong. No matter how I was feeling, I had to go on.

Chapter 28

2000

While playing the piano in the ample lobby of the *Ambos Mundos* Hotel, a middle-aged female customer wearing a summer dress approached me. I smelled her fruity cologne.

"Do you know how to play *Bésame Mucho*?" she asked.

"Yes, of course!" I said with a big smile.

I began to play the customer's requested song, and she deposited a dollar in my tip jar. "Thank you," I said.

I felt comfortable playing at this historic hotel, which once attracted many Americans, including Ernest Hemingway, who lived on the fifth floor in the 1930s. He finished his book "Death in the Afternoon" in this hotel and started two other novels. The five-story pink building, located on the corner of *Obispo* and *Mercaderes* streets in Old Havana, was hard to miss and only three kilometers (two miles) from my apartment in *Centro Habana*.

I rode my bicycle to work and freshened up upon arrival. I carried my best pair of heels, a raincoat, a dress, a Russian cologne, and deodorant in my bag. No one wanted to be near a smelly pianist or one who didn't dress appropriately. However, I had to take good care of my performance attire. I could not just go to the store and buy a new one. Not that I would even if I could. I took diligent care of the clothes I bought when I traveled abroad and never gained any weight, so they still fit me. With all my walking, I was still as skinny as a twig.

Alfredo always accused me of being too thrifty, but if I had not been, I would have never been able to take my mother out of Cuba. I'm sure you understand how important it is to live without regrets, and when it came to my family, I had none. Well, not true. I only wish I had more time with my parents.

I played near the bar and the main lobby's sitting area in an impressive room with soaring ceilings and subdued elegance. The hotel lobby was nearly empty at this hour, but I hoped to see more customers after sundown.

As I played and looked around the room, I noticed a couple and two children sitting in the lobby and another couple behind them. I looked toward the entrance and saw a man entering the building. It could not be! What was Alfredo doing at the hotel? He knew better than to interrupt me when I was at work, so I wondered what had happened.

He approached me, stood near the tip jar, and asked me, "When are you taking a break?"

"Another thirty minutes. Is everything okay?"

"Yes, but I received some news, and I could not wait for you to come home late at night. Besides, I'll be asleep by then."

"Sit down on one of those chairs in the lobby," I suggested.

He walked away and sat near the couple and their two children. As I played, I was restless, wondering what was so important. He had never interrupted my workday before. Was William okay? Was his daughter ill?

Right before my break, the same woman who had requested *Bésame Mucho* returned and asked for a Frank Sinatra song, *New York, New York,* while she deposited another dollar in my jar. I looked in Alfredo's direction. I had no choice but to play what the woman requested, so Alfredo would have to wait a little longer.

At last, my last musical piece ended. I anxiously walked toward Alfredo, who seemed happier than he had been since his wife and son, Alfredito, left in 1997.

I sat next to him with an inquisitive expression.

"What happened? Is everything okay?" I asked.

"Yes, everything is okay, but I was so happy, I couldn't wait to tell you!" he replied cheerfully. "You have no idea how many times I dreamed about this moment."

"Are you going to tell me once and for all?"

"I'm leaving Cuba in a week," he replied.

I felt a knot in my stomach. I could feel the blood rushing to my face, and for a moment, I felt dizzy. Then, I wondered if I had misheard him.

"What do you mean?" I asked, hoping that my ears had betrayed me.

"Alfredito arranged everything. He paid for the legal fees and all the costs. Things moved fast because Anita claimed me. The process goes faster when it comes to husband and wife. So, I will be flying to Miami next week!"

I stared at him expressionlessly. How could *he* be happy? Did he realize what the news was doing to me?

"Aren't you happy?" he asked.

Of course, I wasn't happy. For months, he had been telling me about the progress of the paperwork. However, given that it took Laura twelve years to reunite with her husband, I thought it would be the same in his case. But it had only been three years since Alfredito left, and I wasn't ready to lose another family member to exile.

"Aren't you going to say anything?" he asked.

I inhaled.

"I'm happy for you," I said in a low tone of voice.

"You don't look happy."

"Don't mind me. I have a lot on my mind."

"We should celebrate with a few beers this Saturday with William and some close friends. It will be great!"

"Yes, it would," I replied pensively.

He remained there, looking at me as if waiting for me to say something else. When I didn't, he got up, kissed me, and left. I couldn't move. If I had tried to stand at that moment, I knew my legs would not have been able to sustain me.

I watched him walk away, his footsteps echoing on the tiled floor. Then, I saw him joining the crowd outside the hotel and disappearing among them.

Chapter 29

José Martí International Airport

William, Cecilia, Alfredo, and I stood by the glass-enclosed area at Havana's *José Martí Airport*. Departing passengers waited on the other side of the glass, some in silence.

Since leaving our apartment that morning, I had told myself I would not cry. I would be strong for my brother. His happiness was what mattered most. As he talked about silly things, I gently caressed his face.

"Don't overeat when you get to Miami," I said.

"Are you kidding? After going to bed hungry for so long, I want to eat a big steak. Alfredito is taking me to the Versailles Restaurant when I arrive in Miami."

"Just watch your cholesterol and tell that son of yours to do the same, or the next time I see the two of you, you will be rolling down the streets."

"I'll be fine," he said. "Don't worry so much."

Turning to Cecilia, he added," When I get to Miami, Abuelo will buy you a doll."

"Abuelo, thank you, but I'm too old for dolls. Don't waste your money on that. Just send some food to Tía Milagros, so she doesn't have to work so much."

Eleven-year-old Cecilia had matured beyond her years. She was responsible, studious, and a loving daughter and niece.

"Don't worry. When I get there, I'll find a job and send food as often as possible."

"You worry about yourself," I said. "You know I always find a way. I know that being an immigrant is not easy. I always remember what our abuela Reimunda used to say."

"But she had many children when she and her family arrived in Cuba. Besides, things are different in the United States. I'm ready to work hard."

"You are getting old, Alfredo," I replied. "In only two or three years, you'll be sixty."

"I'm strong; I'll be even stronger once I eat properly."

I didn't want to discourage him, but my next question spilled from my lips before I could stop it.

"What type of work are you going to do? You don't know English?"

"I'll figure something out. You don't have to act like my mom."

"If I don't care for my big brother, who will?"

He laughed.

"Okay, Mami," he said.

We engaged in casual conversation until we saw movement inside the glass-enclosed area. I squirmed next to him and tugged at a lock of my hair. It was time. I took an exaggerated whiff of air, trying to remain calm. I kept telling myself, "My brother's happiness is all that matters. I need to support him."

He looked blissful that day, like someone who had won a million dollars. How could he look so happy when he was leaving so much behind? Our parents' remains were here in the Colón Cemetery. This place kept all our childhood memories: the house in Mantilla where we fought so much, the baseball stadium where we rooted for our favorite team, Havana's waterfront, *El Malecón*, that magical place bathed by the Caribbean Sea. It was a place for dreamers, tourists, and lovers, a gathering place for families, where some sat on the short wall separating the city from the sea, dreaming about the coveted land only ninety miles away. That land's lure was so strong that it was now taking part of me away.

Before he entered the glass-enclosed area, each of us embraced him. I was the last one. When I did, his body felt as thin to me as when he was away in the mountains of Oriente.

"Take good care of yourself, you hear me?" I said again.

"I will," he said before he walked away. I saw him enter the room. My eyes remained fixed on him, his aging body, his balding head, and the white shirt and brown pants that looked too big on him.

When the door opened and exposed the brightness of the runway, he turned around and waved goodbye one last time.

"Goodbye, my brother," I thought as I watched my parents' gift to me walk away. When my parents went to their final resting place, Alfredo had become all that was left of them, the part I thought would stay with me until we were both old and too frail to walk.

I couldn't keep looking in his direction, so I turned toward William and my niece and said, "I'll wait for you at the exit."

I had to walk away before they noticed my weakness, waiting to stream down my face. I didn't want anyone to know how I felt.

I didn't want them to feel the way I did.

Chapter 30

The Elevator

After Alfredo left Cuba, I tried to stay as busy as possible. My nephew William worked all day. When his shift ended, he always had plans. Either he visited his daughter at his ex-wife's house or went out with a friend.

Although I knew many people in Havana, I could count my number of friends on one hand. So, to fight boredom, I accepted whatever jobs came my way. Working as a soloist didn't excite me as much as the camaraderie I found when I played with a group, but the opportunities abounded. I could play at a jazz bar, restaurants, and hotels.

My repertoire had grown over the years. In addition to traditional Cuban music, I played music from Sinatra, the Beatles, Lionel Richie, Billy Joel, and Phil Collins. If I heard a song once, I could duplicate it on the piano. Of course, it wasn't a perfect rendition but a close interpretation of the original.

I worked at two restaurants in the FOCSA Building, *El Emperador* and *La Torre*. The first was on the first floor, and the second was on the 35th floor. Every night, starting at 7 p.m., I played the piano at *El Emperador* for thirty minutes, then took the elevator up to *La Torre* to play for another thir-

The Elevator

ty minutes. That would go on until 11 p.m. I have already told you about *La Torre*, a classy restaurant with the best panoramic views of Havana. *El Emperador* was the opposite: dark and gloomy. I sat at an older, black grand piano and played boleros and soft rock.

Each time I entered the elevator, Manuel, a thin gentleman in his sixties, would greet me with a smile. He had kind eyes, a full head of white hair neatly combed back, and a unique way of making those riding the small elevator feel welcomed.

"Back to the 35th floor, Milagros?" he would ask me.

"You know the routine, my friend."

"I hope the tourists give you nice tips tonight," he would say if no other customers were in the elevator.

"The same with you," I would reply.

"No one gives elevator attendants tips, but that's okay."

"So, how are you doing?"

"When I'm not here, I feel as if all I do is stand in lines and more lines. Isn't that our story?"

"We must remain positive, Manuel. One day, things will change."

"That's what I like about you, Milagros. You have such a positive way of viewing the world. Maybe when you live as long as I have, you will look at the world differently. You are still a baby."

"I'm 49 already. No longer a baby," I said.

"No one would know that unless you tell them. And even if you did, they would not believe you."

I smiled.

The Elevator

"You're always so kind. God bless you."

One day, at the end of my shift, close to 11 p.m., I took the elevator to the first floor.

"So, are you done for the day?"

"I am. My bicycle is waiting for me downstairs."

"It's too late for a young lady like you to be riding a bike alone at this hour."

"I do it every day."

"Please take care of yourself. I want to be able to see you tomorrow."

"I will, Manuel. Don't worry."

We remained silent for a while as I watched the elevator's countdown. Suddenly, it stopped between the 20th and 19th floors.

"Oh my God, what happened?" Manuel shouted. "Hello! Hello! Anyone out there?"

"I think we will be stuck here for a while."

Manuel leaned against the elevator's rear wall and touched his chest.

"I have a problem, Milagros. I'm claustrophobic and have a weak heart. I can't stay here! I need to find a way out!"

He tried to open the elevator's door but failed.

"Oh my God! My wife had warned me not to take this job. But I'm such a hardhead. I'm going to die here tonight." He paced inside the elevator nervously and banged the wall with his fists.

"Anyone out there?" he shouted. When no one replied, he repeated, "I'm dying here tonight."

"No one is going to die, Manuel; please calm down. I'll stay by your side. Don't worry, friend. I won't let anything happen to you. I'll call for help."

The Elevator

After pressing the emergency button, I added, "You see? Help is on the way."

Manuel sat on the floor of the tiny elevator, sweating profusely. He looked terrified, and as the minutes passed, he grew more impatient.

"They are never going to come. I know it!" he shouted.

I sat next to him on the floor and grabbed his hands. They were clammy, and so was his skin. With a calm voice, I said. "I need you to take deep breaths and go to a wonderful place in your mind. Imagine that you are at Varadero Beach with your family."

He ignored me.

"Come on, Manuel. It would be best if you listened to me. You trust me, right?"

He nodded hesitantly.

"Now, deep breaths," I said.

He inhaled.

"Good. That's exceptionally good. I have some water in my purse and a piece of cardboard. You will drink some water first, and then I'll fan you so you can feel better."

He nodded, but I could still see fear in his eyes.

I retrieved the only bottle of water I had left and handed it to him. He took a sip. I didn't know how long we would be stuck here, so I hoped it would last. I fanned him with the cardboard until he signaled me to stop.

"Now, tell me about your wife and children," I said.

"Well, I already told you about my wife. I hope I leave here alive to tell her how right she was."

"What about your children?"

"Well, they haven't been children for a long time. They have kids themselves."

"So, you're a grandfather?"

"Yes, but I haven't seen my grandchildren other than in pictures?"

"Why?"

"I know what you're doing. You're trying to keep me busy so I don't think about what's happening. It's hot in here. Isn't it?"

"Let's keep talking, Manuel. Why haven't you seen your grandchildren?"

"They are in the United States. My sons left Cuba in rafts in 1993."

"Oh," I said and remained quiet, thinking about Alfredo and Angelita's daughters—Laura and Berta—and their children, who now had their own families. I thought about the other family members who had left.

"You too have family in the United States?" he asked.

"Too many," I replied pensively.

We remained silent for a while.

"Milagros, I'll be honest with you," Manuel said. "I don't feel so good. I'm a little dizzy."

"I'll give you more water," I said, checking my watch. I gave him the bottle, and he took another sip. Then, I took a handkerchief from my purse, poured some water on it, and wiped his forehead, but he looked so pale.

The Elevator

"Listen. Why don't you lie down on the floor? I'll lift your legs to increase blood flow to your brain."

"How do you know so much?" he asked.

"I was my parents' caretaker."

Manuel obeyed. After a while, he said, "I feel better now. He then sat next to me.

As we waited, I tried to keep Manuel distracted but was running out of things to say. Occasionally, I would consult my watch, but time seemed to move slower than before.

Finally, we heard a noise outside. It had been an hour since I had pressed the emergency button.

"Hello!" Manuel shouted. "We're here! Can you hear me?"

"Yes! Stay away from the door and stand on the opposite side. Help is on the way."

At last, the elevator's door opened, and we were let out. Manuel hugged me and thanked me. He refused to wait for the elevator to get fixed, so we both took the stairs to the first floor.

"I'm not coming back," he said once we were outside. "Being stuck in that elevator allowed me to think. I want to spend whatever time I have with my wife. She's right. I should retire. My sons help us with food. We don't need much."

"Well, I will miss seeing you every day. It has been a pleasure knowing you," I said.

"Why don't you visit us sometime? It would be great to have a visitor."

Manuel gave me his address, and I wrote it on the cardboard I used to fan him. I also gave him mine.

"You saved my life tonight," he told me. "And I will never forget that. You are a good woman."

"It was my pleasure. Are you walking home?"

"Yes, like I do every night. It's not too bad. About a thirty-minute walk."

"I would take you on my bike if I could."

"Don't worry. I'm used to walking. Well, good night."

"Good night, Manuel."

I smiled, went back inside to change into my commuting attire, and rode my bike home.

Chapter 31

My First Attempt

A few months after Alfredo arrived in Miami, he called me and said he and his wife were separated. He would move to Tampa, Florida, with our cousin Laura, Angelita's oldest daughter, whose husband had died in 1997.

Alfredo told me during telephone conversations that Tampa was an exciting city tied closely to the history of Cuba with its José Martí Park, in honor of the Cuban apostle and poet who fought for Cuba's independence from Spain. It still had several well-preserved red brick buildings in Ybor City that once housed tobacco factories where immigrants from Spain, Cuba, and Italy once worked.

In 2000, around the time when Alfredo moved in with Laura, she was diagnosed with cancer and given six months to live. By then, Alfredo had learned how to drive, but Laura never did, so he would take her to her frequent doctors' appointments whenever her grown children weren't available due to their hectic work schedules.

As you might recall, Laura was one of my mother's favorite nieces, and Alfredo and she always treated each other as siblings, with all the difficulties this relationship brings. Sometimes, they fought with each other, like Alfredo and I used to do. Alfredo would then threaten to leave. She would say she didn't care. Yet, somehow, they worked through their disagreements. I could not believe that these two people, now in their sixties, were behaving again like children.

After Laura's diagnosis, she called me and announced that she was sending me a letter of invitation to the United States so I could visit Alfredo. This was not as easy as it sounded. It required a series of steps and financial commitment. I then realized why my mother loved Laura so much, Laura was so caring. Despite her own struggle with illness, Laura continued to care for others more than for herself.

Laura's daughter, Tania, worked at a hospital in Tampa and didn't take the news about her mother's prognosis lightly. So, she began researching the medical literature, looking for a solution. She learned about a treatment that she thought would help her mother. Luckily, Laura's doctor took a leap of faith and acquiesced in Tania's request for that treatment. At the time, there was not much known about Laura's rare form of cancer. After the doctor began administering the shots to Laura, she improved dramatically. These treatments would allow her to live for years. I realized then that Tania was as optimistic and stubborn as I was.

Despite Laura's best intentions, the letter of invitation was not approved. I still hoped to find a way to visit Alfredo one day, and like Tania, I had no plans to give up.

Chapter 32

Francisco

People say that, sometimes, when a door closes, God opens a window.

Near the end of 2000, William told me that he, too, was leaving Cuba. "Once I arrive in Miami, I plan to work hard to get my daughter out," he said.

I felt numb, realizing that soon, I would be left alone, except for a third cousin I sometimes visited. Two weeks after I said goodbye to William, my life became stale, and a general malaise settled in. I started to feel that my life was meaningless. William's daughter had her mother and stepfather, so I didn't have anyone to worry about or to work for. What was the point of working so hard? Still, I had to do something to keep myself occupied.

For the next several months, I tried to develop a new routine. I would sit on a bench at a park to talk to strangers. Sometimes, I would walk to Havana's waterfront to watch the people go by. But even among large crowds, I felt lonely. Luckily, other people came into my life to make it a little less ordinary. One of those people was Francisco, whom I won't pass judgment on. If my mother had been alive, though, she may have had severe reservations about me becoming friends with someone like him.

Here is how we met. In 2002, I was working at the *Dos Mundos Hotel* during lunch when an elegant, elderly gentleman with so many last names I cannot remember approached me and asked for a song. He deposited one Euro in my jar and stood by the grand piano, watching me. As I played, I noticed his expensive-looking white shirt and smelled his musky cologne.

He applauded happily when I finished.

"It's superb! It amazes me how you can make this piano come to life. You are so talented that you make every fiber within me vibrate to your music."

My face reddened. To this day, flattering remarks make me nervous. I don't think I'm deserving of them.

From that day forward, Francisco and I became friends. He would come to see me play and give me excellent tips.

One day, he visited me in my apartment in Centro Habana.

"I want you to teach me how to play a romantic song for my girlfriend," he said.

"Where does your girlfriend live?" I asked.

"Right here in Havana. Idalia is her name. She's young, you know?"

"How old is she, if I may ask?"

"If I tell you, you will call me an old fool."

We sat in the living room in rocking chairs across from each other. When I didn't reply, Francisco added, "She's much younger, so I'm embarrassed to tell you. I'm seventy years old but tired of being alone."

"Come on. You can tell me. How old is she?"

"Seventeen," he replied.

I remained silent but had difficulty hiding my state of shock.

"I know what you think. She could be my granddaughter, but she makes me feel alive. Every time I look at her, Cuba, Spain, and Africa all come alive in her big brown eyes. You know? Due to my profession, I have had many women but never settled with just one."

"What is your profession?"

"I don't do it anymore, but I was a popular bullfighter in Santander."

"A bullfighter? It is the first time I've met one. Sounds scary."

"I know. Any of those encounters could have ended my life. But I was poor. Becoming a bullfighter became my ticket to fame and fortune. You should have seen my elaborate suits. Women loved them, and I loved women, but I had a weakness."

"What do you mean?"

"I like young women. If they were eighteen, they were already too old for me."

I had heard about men like these but had never met one. I could imagine all the adjectives my mother would have given him.

"Francisco, I would have never thought of you as a man who likes so many women, and even less, ones so young. So, what do you do now? Are you retired?"

"Retired? Oh no. Never! I'm an exceptionally talented painter. I can meticulously replicate the works of the greatest artists, like Da Vinci, Monet, and Botticelli. So much so that experts can't tell the difference!"

"I see. So, you are a man who constantly seeks danger. Won't that get you in trouble?"

Francisco repeatedly rocked in the chair before replying, "What my clients do with my work is their business."

"Don't you think they could make them pass for the originals?"

"Perhaps. But again, I'm not misrepresenting myself. I do what they ask of me."

"You are an interesting person indeed," I replied. "But where are my manners? I haven't offered you coffee."

"Oh, don't serve me coffee. I can only drink one of those tiny cups a day. I came here to learn how to play a love song for my beloved. That's all."

I smiled, thinking about the only time I was in love.

"I see that you are a man on a mission. Let's go to my old piano, and I will teach you a song."

So, that sunny afternoon, while my opened windows invited sunlight into my living room, I showed Francisco how to play a love song for his beloved Idalia. He repeatedly practiced until he played it perfectly. Before he left, he offered to pay me $20, but I refused. So, he went to a tourist-only store and bought me groceries: powdered milk, chocolate powder, rice, beans, and a few steaks! I could not reject his thoughtful gift, so I offered to cook him dinner.

'I'm taking my girlfriend out tonight," he replied.

"But of course," I said. "What was I thinking? Well, thank you for the groceries. That was truly kind of you."

Francisco returned the following week to bring me a perfume bottle and tell me how much his girlfriend liked the song he played for her. Then, he surprised me.

"I have made a decision," he said.

"What is it?"

"I'm going to marry her. I want you to be the godmother." He meant *maid of honor*, but in Cuba, people called it *Madrina* (godmother).

"Francisco, isn't that too rushed? How long have you known her? This is not my business, but I consider you a friend."

"Three blissful months. But don't try to persuade me to change my mind. You see, I don't have many years left. Whatever time I have left, I want to be happy."

"How do you know how many years you have left?"

"A man knows. I eat all the wrong foods and enjoy life a little too much. You know what they say. All excesses are bad. They shave years away. So, will you be our godmother? It would mean a lot to me."

"Of course," I said. "It will be my pleasure."

Under different circumstances, I would not have befriended someone like Francisco, but beggars can't be choosers, as the saying goes.

In the days and weeks that followed until the wedding, Francisco visited me often, took me out for lunch, and brought me gifts. Most people in my position would have taken advantage of someone

Francisco

like him and asked him for things. I accepted what he gave me, realizing that he needed my companionship as much as I needed his and, of course, his gifts, especially meals at some of the best restaurants in Havana.

146

Chapter 33

The Wedding

When Francisco first told me about the wedding, I imagined it would take place at the *Palacio de los Matrimonios* (Marriage Palace), an ornate three-story building across the *Paseo del Prado* and among all the wedding venues in Havana, a particular favorite of engaged couples. The *Paseo del Prado* is a beautiful promenade with canopied trees, gardens, and statues. It divides Old Havana and *Centro Habana* and is lined by iconic buildings like *El Gran Teatro de la Habana* (Havana's Grand Theater). I thought that participating in a wedding there would be my way of experiencing vicariously through Francisco and his bride, the wedding that Adam and I never had.

But I failed to consider that Francisco and his wife could only get married by an international notary, given that he was a Spaniard.

The wedding would take place at the office of the notary across the street from Coppelia, the ice cream parlor where Adam used to take me. That morning, Francisco arrived at my apartment by nine and brought his groom's attire in a bag. Happiness poured from him as if he were a much younger man. We spent all morning together, talking about our lives, and then he took me to the *Habana Libre Hotel* for lunch.

"Are you nervous?" I asked him as I took a bite of my sandwich.

"It's my first wedding, so perhaps I should be, but I'm not."

"Are you sure this is a good idea? At age seventeen, I didn't know what I wanted. Does Idalia?"

"Idalia may not know what she wants, but I do. I like young women. Once they turn eighteen, they are too old for me."

"Francisco!" I replied as my eyebrows shot up.

"Don't judge me. I never did anything without consent. Do you think I wanted to end up behind bars? Her family agrees with this marriage. It will be good for them, especially now that my bride's father died."

I would have said, "But that still doesn't justify your choices." However, that would not have changed anything.

***

About an hour before the wedding, Francisco and I walked from my apartment to the notary, which was three kilometers away. Francisco wore white pants, a white shirt, and a blue bowtie and carried his white jacket inside a plastic bag folded over his arm.

It was a pleasant April afternoon. As we walked from Zanja Avenue to San Rafael Blvd., Francisco asked me about the buildings and neighborhoods we saw along the way. Zanja was home to the *Barrio Chino* (Chinese neighborhood). We passed buildings in various stages of disrepair, many with peeling paint and mold. Few people walked on the sidewalks, while most preferred walking on the road, competing with motorcycles, bicycles, and the few cars passing by.

Everything changed after we turned to San Rafael Boulevard, where the city exploded with well-maintained restaurants, stores, cafes, and with people walking in every direction.

The bride and her family were already there when we arrived at the notary. I felt uneasy when all eyes focused on us, but Francisco promptly introduced me to the bride's immediate family.

"Milagros!" A woman in the crowd shouted. I looked in her direction. I remembered that face! She was the cafeteria manager at the Ministry of the Interior, the one who used to give me a little extra food.

"What are you doing here?" she added.

"Regla? Oh my God, I hardly recognized you with that beautiful blue dress." We embraced and kissed each other on the cheek.

"I came to accompany Francisco. He asked me to be the godmother. Are you related to the bride?"

"Yes, she is my granddaughter!"

"The one in the pictures you used to show me?"

"Yes! Let me introduce you to her! Idalia, come over here!"

The crowd cleared the way for Idalia to get closer to me. I could see why Francisco had fallen in love with her. Her light chocolate complexion, thin but shapely body, and almond eyes made her look like an African princess.

"My name is Milagros," I said. "My God! Francisco said you were beautiful, but you are even more astonishing than I imagined."

Her coral-full lips flashed a smile that brightened the room. "Francisco loves to exaggerate," she said with a soft voice that sounded almost musical.

"This is the pianist I told you about!" Francisco said. "And you see Milagros? I wasn't lying when I told you how beautiful Idalia is."

Idalia nervously played with the long, black curls cascading over her bosoms like party streamers.

"No, you weren't."

"Everyone!" Regla said. "It's time to start the ceremony. We have guests waiting at *La Maison*. You can talk as much as you want during the reception."

"The boss has spoken," Francisco said.

Moments later, the ceremony started. I stood near Francisco and couldn't take my eyes off the couple. Although he was in shape, the age difference was very noticeable. I kept thinking about the desperate situation this family must be in that would compel them to allow such a wedding.

Francisco's eyes stayed focused on his bride most of the time. On the other hand, she devoted most of her attention to her mother and grandmother. The few times she glanced at him, she quickly looked down at the tiled floor, which exposed her long eyelashes and the delicate silver color over her eyelids.

When the notary announced, "You can kiss the bride," I felt a knot in my stomach. Francisco grabbed his bride around her thin waist and gave her a long, passionate kiss, but I could sense her discomfort when one of her arms stayed by her side while the other held on to Francisco's shoulder as if holding onto a cane. Everyone cheered and happily congratulated them. The photographer then took a few pictures to commemorate the occasion, and Regla announced that it was time for the reception.

Francisco spared no expense. The reception was held at *La Maison*, a luxurious mansion built in 1946. Its original owners left Cuba after Castro's rise to power, so the mansion was converted into a guest house. Then, in the 1990s, it was turned into a house of fashion. The mansion had event rooms, a piano bar, a cafeteria, boutiques, and a pool area with a stage where fashion shows were held, often at night.

The wedding reception took place inside, near the piano bar. About fifty people were in attendance, mostly family and friends of the bride.

Francisco had invited a singer who sometimes performed with me at the hotel, so after everyone enjoyed a tasty meal of moist yellow rice and chicken with a fresh salad and white wine, followed by a delicious serving of the wedding cake, Francisco asked for everyone's attention.

"Ladies and gentlemen," he said. "This is an extraordinary day for me. Special days are made even more singular by the presence of extraordi-

nary people. So now, I invite my dear friend and remarkable pianist, Milagros, and the superb singer Antonio to delight us with their music."

I wasn't expecting this, but I shyly rose and walked up to the piano, followed by Antonio. As I played a few boleros, Francisco danced with his bride, surrounded by about a dozen couples.

After the reception, Regla took the microphone.

"I would like to thank everyone for joining us on this exceptional day. The bride and groom will now go to their hotel, and tomorrow, early in the morning, they will travel to Varadero Beach, where they will spend seven blissful honeymoon days."

Later, as I was walking back home, I wondered how long this union would last. I wondered if I would see Francisco again.

Chapter 34

Family

What is family? Is it only those who happen to have our blood? I kept asking myself those questions after meeting Francisco. Frankly, I thought I would not see him again. But I was wrong.

Three days after his honeymoon started, he came to see me.

When I opened the door, I asked, "What are you doing here?" He had told me he had made a seven-day reservation at a Varadero Beach hotel.

"May I come in?" he replied, taking off his white hat before entering my apartment.

"Yes, of course. You're scaring me!"

We sat in rocking chairs across from each other. I offered him coffee, but he once again rejected it.

"You will tell me, 'I told you so,'" he said calmly.

"What happened?"

"Idalia started to cry after two days at Varadero Beach. She said she missed her family, so we had to cut short our honeymoon."

I remained quiet. Why throw a bucket of water over a wet street?

"I don't know what she was thinking. My goal was to bring her to Spain with me. What then? I can't return to Cuba every time she misses her family. What would you do?"

"It's difficult for me to opine, but I think you should give her time. Show her your kindness. She may not love you now, but if she sees you treating her and her family with that true love you say you feel for her, she might change her mind."

I didn't believe my words, but Francisco came to me as a friend to find a sliver of hope, even if he, too, realized his marriage would not last.

The next day, he invited me to lunch. I was surprised when he arrived at my apartment with his young wife and two of her teenage friends.

Later, as we walked down the street toward San Rafael Boulevard, Idalia and her girlfriends remained a few meters before us while Francisco and I followed them like two supervising adults.

"Can you believe this? She doesn't respect me. There she is, walking with her friends while I'm here alone. For God's sake, you act more like my wife than she does."

I inhaled as I glanced at a young couple passing by.

"I hate to be so blunt, but what did you expect? I know how much you love her, but she's a child. Did you believe she married you for love?"

"I know she didn't. I'm not that naïve, but I like to get what I pay for. She owes me the respect I deserve. Allowing me to deflower her was only part of the deal."

His words and selfishness sickened me. I wanted to turn around at that very moment. But I didn't. Maybe God had placed me here for a reason. I didn't know why God crossed my mind on this day when it had not happened for years. My mother believed in him, baptized me, and took me to church until after my Confirmation. After Castro came to power, however, believing in God was frowned upon, so we stopped going to church. Now, I sensed that I needed His guidance.

"Francisco, you cannot view this relationship like a business transaction. You were poor once and did what you could to escape that situation. You should feel compassion for this family."

He stared at me for a moment. I wondered what he was thinking. Was he angry at me?

"That's why I value your friendship," he said. "You make me a better person. I must sound like a horrible man to you. I'm just so lonely. All that money to end up alone."

I sensed he was being truthful, but he looked so defeated.

"Have you thought of showing her that vulnerable side of yours? She needs to see you like a human, not a bank account."

He remained silent for a moment. Then he said, "I keep talking about myself and my problems, but you have more problems than me. Have you heard from your family in the United States?"

His question brought a smile to my lips.

"My brother has turned into the brother I always wanted," I said, thinking about how much I wanted to see my brother. "He calls me at least twice a month and is always concerned about my well-being. He found a job cleaning floors at a large hospital in Tampa. He uses special equipment to clean and likes it there. He is still living with our cousin Laura, but she is helping him find an apartment for low-income people. You know, in case she dies. She is still fighting cancer. He's excited about the possibility of living alone and having me visit him one day. Sadly, it took us being apart for so long to realize how lucky we were to have each other."

He appeared to be analyzing what I said.

"I'm lucky to have you as a friend," he replied, and we continued our stroll toward the restaurant.

Chapter 35

Godmother

It took Francisco six months to obtain permission from the government for Idalia to leave Cuba. During this time, at his request, I accompanied him to several official interviews aimed at determining whether he and Idalia had other reasons than love for marrying each other. The age difference alone would have been enough reason to deny permission, but Francisco was relentless. Still, the favorable outcome made me wonder if he had paid off his interrogators.

Once the flight arrangements were made, Francisco's excitement was noticeable. He even invited me to the *Habana Libre Hotel* for lunch to celebrate.

Days later, when he and his bride were to leave Cuba, I accompanied Regla to José Martí Airport to say goodbye to her granddaughter and Francisco. The rest of the family had said their goodbyes before Idalia left home that morning. Regla told me that the girl's mother wanted to come, but after losing her husband, it would be too difficult to watch her only daughter leave. "She is under psychiatric treatment," Regla told me in reference to Idalia's mother.

Godmother

"You're going to love Spain," Francisco told Idalia with excitement. The young woman smiled shyly. She looked nervous. I could only imagine what she felt. Leaving everyone she loved behind to go to a new country had to be the most difficult decision of her life.

"Francisco, please take care of my little girl," Regla told him. "I would die if something happened to her."

"She will live like a queen," he replied. "I promise."

That day, Idalia wore a long, colorful summer dress and sandals. Her long, curly hair was held back in a ponytail, making her delicate features more apparent. As she kissed her grandmother on the cheek, she shed a few tears.

"I will miss you so much," she said. "Tell Mom not to be sad. In a few months, I can visit you."

Francisco looked at me when she said this. I had told him this would happen. He would not be able to remove this young woman from those she loved and expect her not to want to return.

"Well, it's time for our flight," Francisco said.

He gave Regla and me quick hugs and grabbed Idalia's well-manicured hand.

While the couple walked away, Idalia turned around one last time and threw a kiss at her grandmother. By then, Regla was inconsolable, so I gave her a long hug.

"I feel so guilty," Regla said. "My little girl is doing this for us."

I was shocked to hear her say this, even though I knew it all along.

Godmother

***

I wondered if I would see Idalia and Francisco again, but even if I didn't, I was glad to have met them. They added color to my life when I needed it most.

After the couple left, I returned to my old life. Alfredo continued calling me often to tell me about life in the United States. He loved Tampa, Florida. But occasionally, he would drive to Miami to see his sons.

So, I kept working at the *Dos Mundos Hotel* and going out with friends as much as possible. For three years, I didn't hear anything from Francisco. Then, one day, in 2005, that changed. I was so wrapped up in my thoughts that I ignored the older gentleman pushing a stroller carrying two identical infants with a much younger woman by his side. That was until he called my name.

"Milagros! You have not changed a bit since we last saw you," he said, standing close to the piano.

I happily rose from my bench and embraced each of them. I could not believe my eyes.

"But it can't be!" I said. "And who are those adorable babies?"

"They are my twin sons!" he said proudly while Idalia giggled.

"Francisco, you never fail to surprise me. They are adorable! And you, Idalia, haven't gained an ounce."

"I did gain a few pounds," she replied.

"But you hide them well. So, what are you doing in Cuba?" I asked.

"I wanted to visit my family," Idalia responded, looking far more assertive than the last time I had seen her. "And we also wanted to baptize our twin boys, Odilio and Fernando, here in Cuba."

"And that is where you come in," Francisco added happily.

"Me? I'm not a priest!" I said.

"No, but we want you to be the godmother of one of our children."

I was in shock. What could I do for their children when we lived a vast ocean apart?

"Are you sure you want *me* to be the godmother?"

"We are," he replied. "You have been like a sister to me."

"Francisco, you honor me with your words. I will fulfill that role with pleasure."

The couple sat to watch me play a couple of songs. Then, they had to say goodbye because they needed to go back to their hotel to feed the babies. We agreed to stay in touch until the day of the infants' baptism.

After they left, I went back to playing the piano, beaming with happiness. God had taken everything away from me but had given me this family. Still, I missed my brother terribly, and their joy reminded me of what I didn't have. It also reminded me of Adam. It was 2005, and I still preserved his picture. As silly as it sounded, I looked at it occasionally and thought about the blissful time I spent with him. I knew I would never see him again. However, no one could take away the memories of the happy moments we had together, nor the experiences my family and I shared.

Chapter 36

Purpose

After Odilio's and Fernando's beautiful baptism at the *Iglesia del Sagrado Corazón,* a church built in 1923 in the Gothic Revival architectural style, Francisco and his family returned to Spain but promised to visit Cuba at least every other year so that the family could be closer to the children.

I was happy for Idalia and her family and hoped that my conversations with Francisco had led him to become a better husband than he would have been. That experience changed me in ways I didn't expect. I realized that although I was alone, I didn't have to feel lonely. I just needed to find my purpose.

Playing the piano was one of the reasons for my existence. It made others happy or helped them remember good times with a loved one. I also hoped it made the tourists' vacations a little more special. At least, it seemed so when I saw them doing their best to keep up with the Latin rhythm of *Son De La Loma,* a beloved mid-tempo Cuban song. But I must tell you the story about that song because it illustrates how, if one watches for signs, what we are meant to do reveals itself. This song's composer, the respected Miguel Matamoros, was born in Santiago de Cuba, on the eastern portion of the island. One day, he was performing at the *Colonia Española Hospital* in Santiago when a girl asked her mother, "Are these singers from Havana?" The mother replied, "No, they are from here, from Santiago, from the hills (lomas)." That night, Matamoros finished the lyrics for a song that would make history. The original title of the song was *Mamá, Son de la Loma*. The Trio Matamoros recorded it in New Jersey in May 1928 under *Son de la Loma*, one of the most well-known Cuban songs.

I wanted to keep uncovering my other purposes in life and leave a mark, just like Matamoros did.

The next person who I could help was my brother. The more I spoke with Alfredo, the more I realized how much he needed me. In some ways, I had taken my parents' place. He told me about his job, the woman he had dated for a while until he realized that he preferred to be alone, and his plans to remain in Tampa.

"Why don't you move to Miami with your sons?" I asked him.

"I like my new apartment. Besides, I don't want to live at anyone else's house. Here, I'm in charge."

He also told me that our cousin Laura needed his help while she dealt with her frequent doctor's visits.

In 2006, Alfredo called me unexpectedly one rainy evening.

"I thought you were calling me this Saturday?" I said when I picked up the handset.

Purpose

"I couldn't wait! I received my United States citizenship, so now I can travel!"

I don't cry often, but the news brought tears to my eyes. After being apart for six years, my brother and I would be reuniting again, even if for a short visit.

"When are you coming?"

"I have to ask permission at work and get everything ready, so I am hoping that I can be there in about four to six weeks."

"How long will you be here?"

"Two weeks," he replied.

For the next few days, I was glowing with happiness, making a mental note about all the things I wanted to do with my brother when he arrived. My parents were no longer here, but in a way, they were in the memories enclosed in our Mantilla home—the house my father built, in the stadium where we all had sat together to watch our favorite baseball team, and at the hotel where my father worked. I would help my brother reconnect with his past, and then, he would understand why I was still here and why I couldn't just walk away and leave all the memories behind.

I was in such a good mood during the days prior to my brother's arrival that I started to go out with Julio. The medium-built man with thinning hair was divorced and worked at the hotel. It had not been the first time he had asked me to go to a movie with him, but each time, I had said no. Although I was fifty-five, I feared getting hurt again, like I was when Adam and I had to break up. Granted, the situation was different. Julio was not going anywhere, but what if he did? Then I thought that all I had to do was to make sure not to get too close to him emotionally.

We went out three times in one week. So far, so good. He was easy to talk to. His marriage had broken up because he had found his wife with another man. At least, it wasn't him who caused the marriage to end. Every time I went out with Julio, I felt I was fulfilling my purpose: to make him feel less lonely. I wondered why, out of all women, he had chosen me. I was nothing special; I was still skinny as a twig but had more wrinkles now.

When he offered to accompany me to the airport on the day of my brother's arrival, I hesitated. We had only been together for a month, and it was too soon to introduce him to family. But he seemed as excited as me about Alfredo's visit, possibly because most people in Cuba loved to be visited by foreigners. They loved to hear about their lives and lived vicariously through them. After much thought and discussion with Alfredo, I decided to take him with me.

Chapter 37

Alfredo's Visit

I had not seen any pictures of Alfredo for six years, but I was confident I would recognize him despite the passage of time. On the day of his arrival, my boyfriend (or rather, my life companion), Julio, and Mayda, a cousin I had mentioned earlier (the one who was stuck in Russia for a few weeks after communism fell), accompanied me to the airport.

I considered wearing a pretty dress to welcome my brother, but I didn't want to look awkward, so I chose a white pair of pants and an embroidered blue blouse.

"You look nervous," Julio said as we stood in the middle of the waiting area, surrounded by other families. Mayda giggled.

"Why would you say that?" I asked.

"You haven't stayed still since the moment we arrived."

"You can't blame her," Mayda observed. "Six years is a long time." Mayda understood, as she, too, had lost her half-sister to exile.

We remained quiet for a long while. On any other day, I would have filled the silence with senseless comments just to spark conversation, but I felt too anxious. At last, in the distance, I saw a group of passengers with their luggage, walking toward the waiting area.

"His flight arrived," I said as I examined each of the men in the crowd.

After over twenty people had passed by us, I became more concerned.

"Where could he be? I hope he didn't miss his flight."

"Of course, he didn't. Be patient," Mayda said, tucking strands of her long hair behind her ears. Mayda was pretty and petite, the daughter of my uncle Macho, one of my mother's brothers. That was what everyone called him, so I never knew his real name.

We stayed in silence for a while, watching the passengers go by. I saw families around me embracing their loved ones and crying. "I missed you so much," I heard someone say.

"There he is!" Mayda shouted, pointing toward someone in the crowd.

"Where?" I asked.

"Right there! The guy with the blue shirt and the baseball cap."

"That's not my brother! Is it?"

"Yes, it is him!" Mayda insisted.

Could it be him? As he came closer, I noticed his smile. It was him! I could hardly recognize him. He must have gained about forty pounds and dressed better than men on the island.

"Alfredo!" I shouted and ran toward him. My flat shoes echoed on the floor as I approached him. A few more steps, and I would be able to give him the hug I dreamed about. I had waited so long for this moment.

When he saw me standing in front of him, his smile broadened, and he dropped his long gusano duffel bag. We got lost in a warm embrace.

"I missed you so much," I said.

"I missed you too!" he replied. This time, I knew he meant it, which caused a couple of reluctant tears to escape from my eyes. Mayda and Julio had stayed behind to give me a private moment with my brother.

"Are those Mayda and your boyfriend Julio?" he asked.

"You remembered his name!" I observed.

"I do. Is it serious?" he asked.

"We are friends. Loneliness has an ugly face."

"I can understand that. So, what do you have planned?"

"Let's go home, drop off your luggage, and I want us to visit our parents at the cemetery. Mom needs to see that you're okay."

His brows furrowed as he gave me a curious stare.

"Don't look at me that way. I'm not crazy, but I do go to the cemetery often to talk to them. It must be my imagination, but I feel their presence there more than when I'm at home."

He inhaled. "I understand," he said instead of laughing at me like the Alfredo of the past would have done. His reaction surprised me.

"Well, let's join Julio and Mayda," I said. "Do you need help?"

"No," he replied. "This isn't heavy."

168

As he walked alongside me, I kept turning my head to look at him. I could not believe how much he had changed.

"You look good," I said.

He smiled.

"Thank you. You stayed thin."

"It's not as if I had a choice," I said.

"I sent you food!" he protested.

"I know. It's not about the food. It's about the lines, the long walks to work, and my worries. I don't like depending on anyone."

"You are my sister, and I will always help you," he said. "You don't need to worry about that."

We could no longer continue our conversation because we had now joined Mayda and Julio. Mayda hugged my brother, and Julio shook his hand happily.

"I have heard so much about you," Julio told Alfredo. "I almost feel like I know you."

"I hope it was all good things," Alfredo chuckled.

"Milagros loves you very much," Julio replied. "So, yes, she only says good things about you."

"Not true," I replied. "I also told you that my brother loves to eat, and now, you see what I mean."

"Hey! More respect for your older brother. I'm right in front of you. You can't just call me fat."

"I'm not calling you fat. Even if I called you thin, your stomach would beg to differ."

"There's the sister I know. Always giving me a tough time. Let's go home."

Julio offered to carry my brother's bag. After much insistence, Alfredo gave it to him. Then Alfredo walked by my side and occasionally tapped my shoulder lovingly.

"We'll take a cab home," he said after we exited the waiting area.

Chapter 38

Two Weeks

Two weeks. That was all the time I would have with my brother. And I needed to make it memorable, as I didn't know how long it would be before he could return. There was something special about having him here, next to me. He, the gift my parents left me, encapsulated their essence, and having him by my side helped me feel whole.

"Could you take us to the cemetery after I drop off my luggage at home?" Alfredo asked the driver as we approached my neighborhood.

"It would be my pleasure," Daniel, the white-haired driver, replied.

After Daniel parked in front of my apartment building, Julio helped Alfredo carry his heavy luggage upstairs. When they came back down, Julio said, "Well, Milagros. I need to go back to the hotel. I only asked for a few hours to accompany you to the airport."

Alfredo looked at Julio while he talked to me as if trying to uncover who he indeed was.

"Don't worry," I replied. "I understand."

Julio kissed me on the cheek and shook Alfredo's hand before he left. Alfredo gave him a long, curious stare and firmly held his hand longer than

I would have expected. After letting go of it, Alfredo told Julio, "Take good care of my sister."

"I always do," Julio said.

The tension finally dissipated when Julio walked away.

"Cousin, and I'm leaving too," Mayda said. "You know how busy I am with my parents, work, and the family. That's why we hardly see each other."

"Don't worry," I said. "Thank you for accompanying me to the airport.

"Mayda, please tell your parents that I plan to visit them in the next day or two," Alfredo explained.

Mayda smiled, "They will be pleased to hear that."

Mayda walked away, and Alfredo and I got into the taxi's backseat to begin our journey from *Centro Habana* to *El Vedado*. During our trip, Alfredo commented about the city's deterioration. I didn't say anything. To me, everything seemed the same, as if time had stood still since he left.

Daniel asked Alfredo about life in the United States, and he enthusiastically replied, "It's a wonderful place. You work hard, but you see the fruits of your labor."

"Very different than here," the driver noted. "That's for sure."

We headed south on Pedro Valera Street (Belascoaín-name prior to 1959) and turned right on Salvador Allende Avenue (Carlos III-name prior to 1959). Traffic was light as usual, so it didn't take us long to arrive at our destination. Daniel stopped in front of the elaborate gates of *Cemen-*

terio de Colón, and Alfredo paid him for the trips. Daniel must have been pleased with the tip my brother gave him because he looked at him enthusiastically and said, "If you ever need anything, here is my telephone number. I'll take you anywhere you need."

We thanked Daniel, and he drove away.

"You know, I don't like cemeteries," Alfredo said after Daniel departed. "I'm only agreeing to this because of you."

"I appreciate it. This means a lot to me. You don't have to say anything. Having you by my side is enough. I think Mom would like to see us here together."

He shook his head and chuckled.

"Let's do this," he said.

He was quiet as we walked along sculpted memorials encompassing the 140 acres that made up what is sometimes referred to as *La Necrópolis de Cristobal Colón.* The cemetery, founded in 1876, remained as a testament to Havana's rich culture and history. How could Alfredo have feared being in such a peaceful and beautiful place? The sun was high in the sky now, and its rays were reflected by the marble tombstones all around us.

Silence reigned at this place of eternal rest, except for the occasional sound of traffic outside its gates, our footsteps, and the chirping of birds above.

After we arrived at our parents' tomb, I held Alfredo's hand. I thought he wasn't going to let me, but surprisingly, he didn't push my hand away.

"Mami and Papi, you won't believe who came to visit you today!" I chirped. "My brother Alfredo!

And look at him. Hasn't he changed? I could hardly recognize him."

Turning to my brother, I added, "Alfredo, take off your cap so they can see you better."

Alfredo obeyed while his eyes filled with tears. He looked away for a moment and wiped his face with his free hand.

"He tells me he's happy, Mami. See? You didn't have to be so scared about the family going to the United States. You should see the pictures of Alfredito's son and your great-grandson. He is as handsome as his father. Alfredo is so proud of his grandson."

I paused for a moment to tuck behind my ear a strand of hair that the gentle breeze pushed over my face.

"Alfredo tells me that Laura has cancer, but don't worry. She is receiving good care. Can you believe she has several grandchildren already? The family keeps growing, Mami."

I remained silent for a moment to pay respect to the best parents anyone could have ever had. Alfredo's hands had now turned clammy, and his face reddened. I could see that being here was upsetting him because it reminded him of what we didn't have.

"Well, Mami and Papi," I said after a while. "You know Alfredo. He's always hungry, so we will be leaving now to walk to a nearby restaurant. I don't want Alfredo to pass out. Don't worry; I will continue to visit you to tell you about the family. We love you both very much."

Alfredo let go of my hand after we started to walk away and didn't say anything until after we crossed the front gates of the cemetery.

"So, where do you want to go?" he asked.

It was typical of my brother to hide how he felt after visiting our parents' grave, but I respected his feelings and didn't push him.

"You choose!" I said joyfully.

"Well, you've told me about *El Emperador* before, so let's go there. In most places, customers must pay in dollars. Given that you can't afford to go to any restaurant, this will be a treat for you."

Later, as I sat in front of my brother, I wanted to pinch myself. I couldn't believe he and I were here, at the place where I had entertained tourists so many times. Our waiter recognized me, "Milagros, what are you doing here as a customer?" he asked.

I realized why he was asking the question. It was not a place that I could afford.

"My brother from the United States is visiting me," I said.

"Your brother?" he replied, then lowered his tone of voice and added, "It's a pleasure to meet you, sir. You are a fortunate man."

"Why?" Alfredo asked.

"What else? First, you are lucky to live in the United States. Second, you have a gifted sister. You should see her play the piano. Her sound comes from her soul, and we all feel it. So talented!"

Alfredo flashed a bright smile.

"I'm grateful to live in the United States and to have such a talented sister. She's amazing."

Feeling uncomfortable about the flattering remarks, I looked down shyly.

The waiter took our order and walked away while Alfredo and I stayed in the dimly illuminated, almost empty restaurant.

"So when are you going to allow me to take you out of this place?" Alfredo asked.

I played with my fork and knife. "You know I can't ever leave," I replied.

"But why? I would love to have you near me. We are both getting old and need to help each other."

"As I told you many times, my place is here with our parents and all the memories they left."

Alfredo closed his eyes and his fists as if frustrated by my words. Then, he opened them and spoke calmly, "It is madness to think this way. They are gone. There is nothing left. Please understand that!"

I glanced at him for a long while without responding. He must have interpreted my silence.

"Well, I'm wasting my time trying to convince you. I didn't come here to fight with you. Let's enjoy our time together."

"I'm sure I will," I replied.

Throughout our lunch, I kept wondering if I was wrong. If I were going to leave Cuba, this would be the time to do it when I still had a few productive years ahead. Yet, something held me back. For what was I waiting?

176

Chapter 39

After His Departure

Alfredo's duffel bag from the United States contained food and clothing for me. He also brought a coffee bag for each of our mother's brothers.

We visited our few relatives in Havana. They were always too busy with their problems to have time for anyone else, but Alfredo said it was the right thing to do.

After taking several old taxis, Alfredo said, "I am so tired of smelling like gasoline. I must take cold showers every time I get back to your apartment because I smell like death."

"I don't know what you're talking about. I don't smell anything."

"That's because the part of your brain that senses these odors is dead."

"Are you calling me brain-damaged?"

He laughed, and I laughed with him.

We took a day to visit the house in Mantilla. We were so excited to see it again after all this time, but then reality hit. Its second floor had vanished. The street was now paved, and we had to go around the block a few times to ensure we were looking at the home where we grew up.

"How can it be?" Alfredo said, looking at the unpainted and moldy first floor. "It's destroyed."

I swallowed, unable to comment.

As if to keep hurting myself, we visited the old *Sierra Maestra Hotel* (*Rio Mar* before the revolution), an eleven-story building facing the Caribbean Sea in the Miramar area. This was where it all started. This was where I met the love of my life. It hurt me deeply to see it like this. So run down, with empty, abandoned pools full of dirt and old leaves. Most of the building was uninhabitable, but a few daring families, risking their lives, still decided to make it home. Substantial portions of the first floor appeared as if they had been bombed.

"Is this why you're staying?" Alfredo asked me when he saw me wipe the emotions that rolled down my face. "What do you want, to witness the destruction they are leaving behind?"

His words were like a sword buried into my chest. I looked down, and he must have noticed my sadness because he grabbed my hand and added, "I'm sorry. I shouldn't have."

"I deserve it," I said.

The days with my brother went by too fast. After I said goodbye to him at the airport, once again, I re-lived that sorrow I had experienced the first time. Once again, a part of me had been torn out.

I couldn't go back to work for three days. I didn't want to see anyone. I sat in front of the piano and played *Time in a Bottle* dozens of times. I wanted to spend the time I had left with my brother and my family in the United States. Yet, how could this place keep holding me here, like a curse, like a powerful magnet?

The two small dogs I owned sat by my feet most of the day as if sensing how I felt.

The day Alfredo left, before we lost electrical power, I stood in front of the mirror. I saw a woman with tanned skin and some wrinkles around her eyes, and I didn't recognize myself in her. I knew that the innocent girl full of dreams still lived inside her. But over the years, she had slowly disappeared like footprints along the shore washed away by the waves. Like those footprints, I feared that one day, that girl would disappear completely.

Chapter 40

2013

I was excited to be in an airplane cabin on my way to Tampa, Florida. My brother had talked so much about this place that had been his new home for thirteen years. He spoke about its wide variety of affordable restaurants (he still loved to eat), the unique architecture of the University of Tampa with its iconic minarets, and the historic Ybor City with its popular Columbia restaurant, cobblestone streets, and colorful roosters and hens walking around as if they owned the place. "Those chickens would not have lasted a day in Cuba," Alfredo said during one of our telephone conversations.

Based on the multiple conversations around the cabin, I concluded that the plane was full of people like me who were visiting their loved ones. I imagined that some, like the young woman I saw across the aisle wiping her face, would never return.

The atmosphere inside the cabin was cheerful and lively, even more so after the airplane took off. I had a window seat and kept my eyes focused on the land below, but it quickly disappeared. Then, a symphony of shades of blue took the stage, followed by white, fluffy clouds. I wondered if my parents were somewhere above these clouds in a Heaven that we mortals could not see.

"Traveling alone?" the woman next to me asked me, distracting me from my thoughts.

Then, I realized that this was the first time I had traveled alone, with neither my band members nor my mother.

"I am," I said. From that moment forward, I began to probe the woman, confident that she was a far more interesting person than I was. I felt sorry for her after a while, with all my inquiries, but I needed to kill time and stop thinking about my meeting with my brother and the rest of the family. Strangely enough, that made me nervous.

By now, our Tampa family had lost one of its most beloved members, our cousin Laura, who had taken her last breath in December 2011, surrounded by her three adult children. After fighting cancer for ten years, she stopped taking the injections that kept her alive because the side effects were so much worse than the cancer. She knew her decision would lead to her demise, but she was ready. I respected her for that. She told Tania, her oldest daughter, "It's time."

Laura had seen her three children become successful and contributing members of society. The oldest, Tania, worked as Controller for Tampa General Hospital, the largest hospital in the area. The youngest son, Gustavo, was now part owner of a glass company and an inventor, and Lynette (the middle child) was working for a large hospital system.

Alfredo had told me that each of Laura's children owned their beautiful, well-painted houses debt-free. After having raised them alone in Cuba and then becoming an immigrant, Laura knew what it was like to have nothing. She had passed on her life lessons to her family. "Always live below your means, and you won't have to enslave yourself to debt. Spend little in wants and focus on paying off your house." Her children listened to her and lived thriftily at first, but once they paid off their houses, they began to travel.

Although nervous, I couldn't wait to meet them. But what if they didn't like me? Our plane began its descent around 8:30 a.m. Thirty minutes later, I was inside one of the most beautiful airports I had ever seen. It was immaculate and modern, with various stores and lots of seats.

I was so nervous that I had to stop at the ladies' restroom, so I didn't keep up with the passengers on my flight. After I finished, I didn't know where to go. An elderly woman who I recognized from my flight was in the same situation. We started to walk together until we found an employee and tried to communicate with her. But she didn't understand us. The employee then began to walk with us and asked us to stand in front of a set of sliding doors.

"People mover," she said.

I didn't know what she meant, but then I noticed a little train approaching us.

When the doors opened, she said, "Get on the train." She also pointed toward the train with her index finger.

"What is she saying?" the elderly woman kept asking me.

"Just come with me."

"But where are we going? Where will we get off?"

"I don't know," I said. "We'll figure it out together."

Right before the sliding doors closed, a few more passengers entered the people mover. I was thankful. I would just follow them.

After a short ride, the sliding doors opened, and the group of passengers exited.

"Let's exit," I told the elderly woman.

We walked toward the waiting area. The elderly woman must have seen her family because she shouted, "Cachita, I'm here!"

Four family members rushed toward her and covered her with kisses.

After they left, I was alone. I was lost in this enormous place where I thought no one would understand me if I asked for help. I started to walk toward the escalators when I heard a female voice in the distance.

"Milagros!" I saw a woman waving at me. I looked behind me to make sure she wasn't talking to another Milagros. But no. She meant me.

"I'm Tania," she said when we were in front of each other.

"I'm Milagros," I said nervously, but then I immediately realized I didn't need to introduce myself. "That's right. You already know that."

"Alfredo said you were funny," she said and giggled.

The last time I saw her, she was a thin and shy fourteen-year-old. Now, she was a woman in her forties, assertive, well-dressed, and very welcoming.

"You look great!" she said.

"Stop laughing at me, Tania. You have been around my brother too long. I am skin and bones—that's all I am—107 pounds."

"That's better than my 140."

I waved my hand in dismissal. "You look lovely," I said. She thanked me.

"So, where is my brother?" I added.

"He said he was going to look for you."

"It figures. He's always in *La Luna de Valencia.*" I know this phrase means nothing to you. Valencia's moon is like saying, "on another planet."

I offered Tania my condolences on her mother's death, and we talked about the family and our breathtaking surroundings. Everything looked clean and bright, with tall ceilings and shiny flooring. I could even see a restaurant from where we were standing.

"Milagros!" I heard a male voice say. I recognized it and looked in that direction. There he was, rushing toward me.

"Where were you?" I asked and hugged him.

"Looking for you! Where do you think I was?"

"I was here all along with Tania."

"You weren't here when I started looking for you."

"You need better glasses."

Tania kept laughing, watching us go back and forth like children.

"Well, let's get out of here. We have a lot to do," he said and grabbed my bags.

And he wasn't kidding. Alfredo had prearranged all the activities that we would do over the month that I was going to be in the United

States. He had spent his working years saving money to take me to places I had never seen.

My rollercoaster ride through this magical place called the United States was about to begin.

Chapter 41

The United States

Alfredo had a packed itinerary because he was afraid I would not be able to return to the United States. I wondered if that was his way of convincing me to stay.

After we left the airport, we went straight to the cemetery to see Laura's final resting place. She shared the same plot as her husband, Rio. Alfredo explained that they were stacked one on top of the other to save money. Even until the end, Laura was thrifty.

What a difference between the cemetery in Cuba and the one in Tampa. The one we visited in Tampa had only a handful of tall granite memorials. The rest were on the ground, bronze plaques over granite pieces that were no longer than my forearm, with grassy areas between them. There was no grass at the Colón Cemetery but numerous elaborate memorials, one next to another.

Tania remained silent as she looked at the names on her parents' plaque. Meanwhile, I talked to Laura, as I did when I visited my parents at the Colón Cemetery. "Thank you for giving my brother a place to live," I told her. "Sorry I didn't get here in time to see you. Don't tell your sister when you see her again one day, but you were always my mother's favorite."

Alfredo shook his head and rolled his eyes but didn't say anything.

When we were done paying our respects, I asked Alfredo, "So, what's our next stop?"

"Lunch at Tania's in-laws' house," he said.

In our minds, we said our final goodbyes to Laura and Rio and got back in Alfredo's four-door Chevrolet.

We drove for thirty minutes to a house on Clifton Street, close to Hillsborough Avenue and the airport. "Many Cuban families live in this area," Alfredo explained. They are primarily lower-middle-class houses," he added. However, when I looked at them, they were all painted, and the street was paved. Unlike the houses in Cuba, these had paved driveways and big front yards.

Alfredo turned from the street into the driveway.

"We are here," he announced. Like the others, the house was painted in a neutral color. This one was cream, with an elaborate brown door and a cute tiled front porch with two rocking chairs that reminded me of home.

As if knowing that the front door would be unlocked, Tania didn't knock and went right through, followed by Alfredo and me. Moments later, we found ourselves in the living room. I saw our reflection in the glass wall behind the sectional sofa. I looked like some of the women in Hitler's concentration camps. I was almost five feet and eight inches, too tall for my current weight.

"Madeline, Guillermo, we are here!" Tania announced and asked us to sit on the cozy sofa. In the contiguous dining room, a large table was set that accommodated six people. The aroma of freshly cooked food inundated our senses.

"The food smells so good," Alfredo chirped.

The walls and the small table across from us were full of family pictures, a few of Tania and her husband Phil and the others of children.

"Those are their three grandchildren," Tania explained. She then pointed at her son's picture from when he was little. By now, he was a married man.

Looking at all these pictures made me realize all the experiences I had missed. While I sat in Cuba playing a piano for tourists, stuck in time, life in the United States had passed like a flash of light. This could have been my family. It was my family, yet I felt like a stranger. It was as if I didn't belong.

Madeline and Guillermo, both in their seventies, appeared and greeted me as if they had known me all my life. We rose from the sofa. Madeline was tall, like my mother, and had the same thick and dark hair. Guillermo was about an inch shorter and had tanned skin and small eyes. He had also lost most of his hair.

"Oh my God," Madeline said, embracing and kissing me. "You look so young."

"I know. I'm so skinny; I look like a child."

"Well," Guillermo said with a bright smile. "Get ready to eat because Madeline cooked a great meal."

I played with my hands and looked down. These people were too old to be cooking for me. It should be the other way around.

"That's right," Madeline said. "You must be starving. Come over to the dining room and have a seat."

We obeyed. As she served each plate and gave it to Tania to place on the table, Madeline said, "Alfredo told me so much about you; I feel like I know you."

"I hope it was all good," I said, staring at my brother.

Madeline flashed a kind smile. "Of course, it was. Your brother adores you. He was so excited about your arrival that he made us all excited, too."

Moments later, when Tania placed a giant plate of pork, black beans, rice, and plantains in front of me, I thought I was dreaming.

After everyone sat down, I ate slowly, hoping I could get through the entire plate, savoring the elaborate seasonings almost impossible to find in Cuba.

"So, Alfredo tells me you are a talented pianist," Madeline said.

"I don't know whether I'm talented, only that I am a pianist."

"And what do you like to play?" Guillermo asked. "I like to sing."

"That's right. Guillermo and I sing together in the car when we go to Miami," Tania added.

"Well, I play a variety of songs. *Yesterday*; *New York, New York*; *Love Story*; *Bésame Mucho*;

189

Strangers in the Night; and anything people ask me to play."

"I can't wait to see her playing my piano," Tania said.

The conversation around the table then switched to the growing family. After a while, I noticed that everyone had finished their food, but I still had half of mine left. I didn't want to look ungrateful, but my stomach felt as if it was about to burst. Madeline noticed.

"You don't like it?" she asked.

"I love it, but I'm not used to eating this much," I explained. I didn't tell her I felt like crying when I saw so much food.

"You should try to eat so the food doesn't get wasted," Alfredo said.

I wanted to step on his foot, but instead, I just stared at him.

"Leave her alone, Alfredo," Madeline said. "She doesn't need to eat it all."

"I will give my leftovers to my brother," I suggested.

"I'll eat them," Alfredo said enthusiastically.

"That's why you can't fit into your shirt!" I said, and everyone burst into laughter.

"So, where is your husband, Tania?" I asked.

"At work, but I took the day off," she said.

Tania's kindness touched me deeply. I could tell that she had inherited Laura's thoughtfulness.

After a delicious lunch followed by a piece of flan, we took our conversation to the living room and conversed for an hour over a cup of coffee.

"I would like to be home before rush-hour traffic," Tania said. I wasn't familiar with that concept because there wasn't such a thing in Cuba.

"What is that?" I asked.

"When everyone leaves work around the same time and the roads become impossible," Tania explained.

I thanked Madeline and Guillermo for their hospitality. During my visit, I learned they were simple people. Guillermo worked at the shipyards repairing boats, while Madeline cleaned floors at Hillsborough County Schools. Yet, they owned their beautiful home debt-free and were enjoying a comfortable retirement. If they lived in Cuba, they would have never been able to live like this.

I was starting to understand why so many people risked their lives to be here.

After we left the house on Clifton Street, Alfredo drove Tania and me around Tampa. He showed me the stadium, the huge park across from it, and the West Tampa neighborhood, another predominantly Cuban area. He stopped at Florida Bakery and bought me an éclair.

"Do you want me to blow up?" I asked him.

"God, you're being difficult today," he replied. Tania giggled.

I could not say no to that creamy éclair, so I devoured it. We then headed north towards Carrollwood, where Tania lived. I was looking forward to visiting her house and serenading her with my music.

Chapter 42

Laura's Children

It was almost five when we arrived at Tania's house in Carrollwood. Alfredo parked in front of its two-car garage next to a shiny grey Toyota Camry.

"My husband is here," Tania observed. "He probably left work early."

I was in awe when I looked at my surroundings, from the manicured garden, not only in front of Tania's house but in front of every house on her block, a combination of tall trees, evenly cut shrubs, and well-trimmed healthy grass. It was like a sonata in green.

The house seemed much newer than Madeline's, with a higher-sloping roofline that revealed its brown shingles.

"Wow! You are living large," I said.

Tania laughed.

"You are hilarious. This is not a big deal. There are much nicer houses in Tampa in places like Ávila. My father used to tell me about the mansions he saw there."

"What was he doing there?"

"It was years ago, in the late 1980s. A doctor who lived there asked him to build a glass staircase."

"Glass? Wow. You must really want to throw money away when you ask for a glass staircase. Never mind the additional risk of slipping and falling."

Once again, Tania laughed while she walked toward the entrance, key in hand.

She must have thought I was kidding, but I wasn't. In Cuba, doctors were poor, like everyone else. Well, everyone except those well-connected with the government. That made me think and reconsider what I had said. Maybe I was wrong. If the doctor made his money through years of studying and arduous work, who cares how he spent it? In fact, his idea of having a glass staircase allowed Tania's family to make a living.

At least, in the United States, people like Tania and those in healthcare who applied themselves could achieve a good standard of living. Alfredo told me that Tania had two master's degrees. She and her husband (who had a master's in business administration) had worked extremely hard for what they had. They worked full-time and attended the university at night, all while raising a son.

"Phil, we are here," Tania announced as we entered and proceeded to open the vertical blinds in front of the sliding double doors leading to the large back porch.

"Beautiful house, Tania," I said.

She thanked me as she opened a set of double doors leading to the piano room.

"Oh my God, this is your piano!" I said. "Can I play?"

"I've been dying to listen to you," Tania replied.

The room was furnished with only a sofa and an upright black piano with a handful of family pictures on top. Alfredo and Tania sat next to each other on the couch, and I started to play.

"Breathtaking sound," I said as I played.

"It is!" Tania replied. "My piano never sounded this good."

"I'm referring to the tuning of the piano, not my music."

"And I'm referring to *your* playing. You're superb."

I thanked her and continued to play old Cuban songs, like *"Bésame Mucho,"* songs that I thought she would appreciate. Based on her comments, she enjoyed them. While I played, I didn't realize that Phil had joined Tania and Alfredo and had pulled a chair to watch me.

After a while, I stopped playing, and everyone applauded.

"You are amazing," Phil said.

I quickly rose from the piano's bench.

"Oh my God! You must be Phil. Tania told me so much about you."

Phil, still in his work clothes—a white, long-sleeve shirt and a pair of blue pants—tried to shake my hand. Instead, I hugged him and kissed him on the cheek, which made him feel awkward. I could tell by his nervousness and Tania's giggles.

"I'm sorry. In Cuba, we hug and kiss a lot."

"No worries. I grew up in the States, but I see Mom kissing and hugging everyone. So, I understand."

Phil was much taller than his father but was bald like him. Unlike him, he wore glasses and had a thin mustache. But he had a kind smile.

"So, what are we doing for dinner?" Phil asked happily.

"We are all getting together at Carabba's tonight on Sheldon Road. My siblings and their spouses are joining us to welcome Milagros," Tania said.

"Oh my God. More food?" I asked. "Are you guys trying to kill me?"

They all laughed. I didn't know why people kept laughing at everything I said. I honestly wasn't trying to be funny. I was only expressing what I felt. But everyone ignored me.

I was worried what would happen if I ate more food. What if I burst? My stomach has only so much capacity.

"Where is the bathroom?" I asked.

"The guest bathroom is in the hallway to your left."

"Guest bathroom? You mean you have more than one bathroom?"

Once again, everyone laughed, and I was starting to feel uncomfortable. I wish Alfredo had given all these details before I came, so I wouldn't be as shocked as I was at everything.

The bathroom was like none of the bathrooms in ordinary Cubans' houses. The toilet and sink were shiny and clean, and so were the tile floors. I could not see one broken tile.

As I was there relieving myself, I decided to keep my reactions to myself. After all, I lived in the center of Havana and had traveled abroad. It was not as if I had not seen pretty things. However, I had not visited the people in the places I had traveled, so I was expected to be shocked by these new experiences. But I refused to let people laugh at me, even if they were doing it lovingly.

****

That evening, we met with Tania's siblings and their spouses at an Italian restaurant called Carrabba's. Silly me, I thought that all Italian restaurants included pizza and spaghetti on the menu. And maybe this one did, but Alfredo could not find these items (possibly because his English was not good). So, instead of asking for help, he ordered me a soup. It looked good, but when I tried it, I opened my eyes wide and kicked him under the table.

"What's wrong?" he muttered.

"Spicy!" I whispered, feeling as if my mouth were on fire.

I took a couple more tablespoons, hoping it would get better, but I ended up with blisters. So, there I was, looking at everyone else enjoying their selections while I was trying to do everything possible to conceal the pain.

"Do you like it?" Tania asked.

I enthusiastically nodded without saying anything. Eventually, Alfredo took my soup and gave me a piece of his bread. At least, the pressure to eat it was off.

That evening, I met the rest of Laura's children. Each of them was so different than the next. Lynette, the middle child, had long hair like her sister but was a little heavier than her. However, she carried her weight well. She was cheerful and made jokes about silly things. At least, now those around me could laugh at someone else. She had two children of her own and three stepchildren from her second marriage. Gustavo was as handsome as his father had been. In fact, for a moment, I thought I was looking at Rio. He had tanned skin and strong muscles. Both Lynette and Gustavo were married to people who didn't have a Cuban background and didn't speak Spanish, so I could only communicate with them through gestures.

That night, I noticed that no matter whether one received an education in the United States, there were many paths to success. Gustavo had worked for a glass company for years and was an inventor. He was responsible for the growth that the company where he worked had achieved over the past twenty years. Therefore, he received the same wages as someone with a degree, although he didn't have one. Lynette worked at the same hospital system for over twenty years. She had a retirement plan and made good money even though she only completed a handful of college classes.

Our dinner conversation revealed something I had not thought about for years. Remember the story about the stolen chocolate? I finally found out who ate it. Laura did! Her sister Berta told Tania, and she told us.

After a wonderful evening with Laura's children, I realized that my grandmother Reimunda had been wrong. She should not have made her family so fearful of leaving Cuba. My life would have been vastly different if she hadn't.

Chapter 43

Seven-Day Cruise

Alfredo had told me that he had a packed schedule in store, and he wasn't kidding: a seven-day cruise, a trip to Walt Disney World, and a seven-day vacation in Las Vegas. I thought he had lost his mind. Why would he spend so much money on me? I didn't deserve his generosity, so I told him so.

"Let me do this for you, okay?" he said.

"But why?" I asked.

"I don't need a reason."

It was true that he didn't need a reason, but why so much? But there was no arguing with him. Besides, he had already paid for everything.

The day before our cruise, Alfredo and I drove to Miami, a five-hour trip from Tampa that took us through Alligator Alley. This 80-mile highway stretch crossed the Big Cypress National Preserve and the Everglades, an area teeming with wildlife.

That night, we stayed at Alfredito's three-bedroom apartment, which he shared with his mother and brother William. The apartment complex had multiple buildings and a large entertainment area with a gigantic swimming pool, a gazebo, and a heated spa. The area around the pool boasted several tables, chairs, and umbrellas.

The apartment was beautifully furnished. Its cozy living room included a cream-color leather sofa with a matching loveseat and decorator pillows and a glass table with a fancy floral arrangement. Across the table, an entertainment center featured a large television set. That night, we sat around the television, ate pizza, and drank beer.

The next day, Alfredito and William drove us to the Port of Miami, where we joined our cousin Magaly. While I was in Cuba, I spoke with her a few times by telephone but did not see her in person until the day of the cruise. Although she was my age, she looked as if she were in her fifties. She had fair skin, dark hair, and a pretty smile. Magaly—approachable and fun to be around—worked for the cruise industry and had traveled all over the world.

That sunny Sunday, when Alfredo, Magaly (who also lived in Miami), and I boarded the Royal Caribbean ship at the Port of Miami, we looked like tourists. We wore straw hats, glasses, shorts, and T-shirts. After the cruise employees took our pictures, we boarded the multi-story and impressive modern ship. I had never seen anything like it. However, I kept my emotions in check. I marveled at my surroundings inside my head and acted as if it had not been my first cruise, as if I were used to all the things happening around me.

The cruise would take us to Dry Tortugas, Punta Cana, and Montego Bay (Jamaica).

Our "inside" cabin (the least expensive option) was not ready, so Alfredo suggested we go to the cafeteria to eat lunch. Magaly had a late breakfast, so she went to catch some sun on the deck.

Alfredo told me while we rode the glass elevator, "You will love this! There is a broad selection of not only foods but also desserts. And as much as you want."

When he spoke, happiness radiated from him. I felt terrible for this man, who had deep grooves between his eyebrows and under his cheeks and wrinkles around his eyes. It was as if he was trying to make up for the way he treated me when I was a child. But he didn't have to. He didn't understand that true love was forgiving and blind to imperfections.

"You are a good brother," I said. "I won't ever forget what you're doing for me."

He flashed a broad smile. I could not believe how much the years had changed him. He was seventy years old but still looked handsome. Although he loved to eat, he walked every day and kept up with his doctors' appointments. He lived in an apartment complex for low-income seniors right off the Hillsborough River in Tampa. So, every morning, he sat outside with a cup of Cuban coffee and looked at the river and its surroundings, at the lush greenery and variety of birds that made their home around that area. That was the apartment that Laura had helped him find during her last years of life so he would have an affordable place to live. Because of Laura, Alfredo had been able to save money to treat me to vacations like this one.

When the elevator doors opened, I could hear cutlery, plates, and multiple conversations. A large group of people waited by the set of elevators. The dining room was so packed that Alfredo suggested we find a place to sit first. We had to walk around the multiple sitting areas until we found two empty seats.

"Stay here. I will get our food. What are you in the mood for?"

I shrugged.

"I don't know. I don't eat very much. Whatever you think is best. Just don't bring me too much. I prefer to save space for desserts."

"Sounds great!"

Alfredo returned twenty minutes later carrying a tray with two plates full of a variety of foods, some of which I didn't recognize.

"What is the orange stuff?" I asked.

"Sweet potato?"

"That doesn't look like any sweet potato I know," I replied.

"It's an American sweet potato. It's quite different from the Cuban one, not only in taste but also in appearance and consistency. You will love it."

I tried it and liked its texture and flavor even more when I ate it with hamburger meat and a piece of chicken. I gave Alfredo what I didn't want, and he happily took it.

"I'm a little full and need to leave room for dessert," I said.

"That's fine. Did you like the sweet potato?" he asked.

"It was tasty."

Alfredo stayed in his seat while I went for my desserts. I lost control when I saw the variety of colorful tiny cakes. So, I took three small ones and topped them with ice cream. Alfredo then went for his. He returned with four of them and topped them with ice cream as well.

"If our parents could watch us now," Alfredo said.

"Maybe they are," I replied.

After lunch, we went outside to the pool area, where people gathered to enjoy drinks and music. There, we reconnected with Magaly, who was enjoying a hamburger and a Coke near the pool.

Three hours later, after our cruise ship left the port, we went to our cabin, gathered our life vests, and got ready for the safety drill.

Our adventure at sea then began. I had never been on a ship before, and our large ship looked tiny in comparison to the immensity of the ocean. During one of our days at sea, I sat outside and thought that somewhere beyond those waters was Cuba. That island kept my parents and grandmother's remains, and it witnessed so many happy moments in my life (and sad ones, too).

But I didn't want to be sad. I wanted to enjoy this cruise with my brother and Magaly. So, every day, Magaly would read us the program for that day, a document containing the timing for each of the activities on the ship. Each day, we attended as many of the ship's games and shows as we could.

During port days, I was pleased to discover that Punta Cana (in the Dominican Republic) and Montego Bay (in Jamaica) had the same tropical feeling as Cuba, with their impeccable sandy beaches and lush tropical vegetation. The beach resorts we visited were much fuller and better maintained, and the music was different—primarily Jamaican-style sounds.

During one of the last evenings, as we were bordering the western tip of Cuba, on the way back to Miami, our ship began to rock wildly. We had just finished our dinner, but another group was coming in, and we heard glasses and plates hit the floor. I got so scared.

"Are we going to be okay?" I asked.

"We have an experienced crew," Magaly said. "They know what to do."

Luckily, we were wearing patches for motion sickness, but those passengers who didn't pay the price.

"We should go toward the middle of the ship," Magaly suggested. "There is usually entertainment there."

We listened and sat on comfortable chairs to watch an exceptionally talented piano player. The piano sounded so good that it made me forget about the rocking ship for a while. After the waves pounded our ship for an hour, the captain announced that due to severe weather, he would need to turn the ship around and wait for the storm to pass.

Despite the harsh weather, the ship's activities weren't canceled. I was impressed by the talent of the shows' singers and dancers and the crews' emphasis on customer service, something I had not experienced before.

The following day, we arrived in Miami as scheduled. Magaly told me that in the middle of the night, the weather improved, and the captain was able to turn the ship around again.

As we disembarked, I thanked Alfredo again for giving me such beautiful memories.

"Thank Magaly, too," he said. She passed her discounts on to us." I thanked her and smiled, thinking about my parents. They had taught us to be thrifty. Even as Alfredo showed his generous spirit, he had done so at the lowest cost possible, and I applauded that.

I looked forward to discovering other magical places where Alfredo planned to take me.

Chapter 44

Walt Disney World

The day after our cruise ended, Alfredito drove his son Andy (who was almost a teenager), William, Alfredo, and me to Orlando, Florida, to visit Walt Disney World.

"So, why are you taking me to Walt Disney World?" I asked Alfredo.

"The real reason?" he asked.

"Of course!"

"He was a dreamer, like you. So, I thought you would like to see this place."

"Is it a bad thing to be a dreamer?" I asked.

"Once I thought it was, but not anymore," he said. The world needs more people like you."

Alfredo wasn't acting like the brother I knew. The years apart had changed him.

Andy was so excited.

"You will love all the rides!" he told me, his brown eyes growing wider with excitement.

"I'm sure I will," I said.

We encountered heavy traffic on I-95 but arrived at the park only thirty minutes later than expected.

Upon arrival, we stood at the end of one of the long lines that resembled the ones in Cuba when chicken arrived at the bodegas, with the exception that these lines moved much faster. When we entered the park, I felt as if I was in a fairy tale. The music, the joyous atmosphere, the beautiful castle in the middle of the park, and the Disney characters—which brought smiles to children's and adults' faces alike— overwhelmed me.

The creators of this park paid attention to every detail, from the manicured gardens to cheerful music that made me feel like a child.

"Let's go to the Space Mountain ride first," Alfredito suggested.

As we walked through the amusement park on our way to this ride, no one gave me details about it. Later, while we stood in another lengthy line to enter Space Mountain, the excitement built up.

"I love this ride!" Alfredito said. Andy and William echoed his feelings.

"When there are so many people waiting, it must be good," I said.

"It's great!" Alfredito replied and elbowed William. William smiled wickedly, which told me that he and his brother were up to something. I just didn't know what, and Alfredo was too distracted watching the families around us to notice.

Soon, I would know what my nephews had in store for me. They asked me to take the first seat. A few minutes later, I realized that this was not a clever idea. William sat behind me, followed by Alfredo.

"Hold on tight, Tía Milagros," William said before the ride started.

"What do you mean?" I asked. But before he replied, we started to move. Moments later, we

206

were enveloped in darkness and going at full speed. I could hear people screaming but could not see anyone. I held on for dear life, unable to get a word out. My heart was pounding, and the palms of my hands turned sweaty. I also had an urgent need to use the restroom.

"Yay! Do you like it, Tía?" William shouted.

"Of course not!" I yelled frantically. "Why didn't you tell me it was fast?"

I could hear him laughing. "Come on, Tía. It's fun! Yay!"

I closed my eyes and tightened every muscle in my body, consumed with fear and unable to say anything else. At one point, I sensed a flash. Then, the ride ended. I felt a little dizzy when I got off.

"Come on, Tía Milagros, it wasn't that bad," William said.

"You and your brother knew how fast it was and didn't tell me," I said. "That is not right. You should have warned me."

Alfredito and his son got off the ride and joined us.

"It was fun, Tía. Wasn't it?" Alfredito said, giggling.

"It wasn't fun! It wasn't fun at all!"

"We didn't know you were scared of fast rides," William said.

"Let me ask you, William. How old am I? When have I been on a ride like this? It's not difficult to figure it out. I thought I was going to have a heart attack. You almost killed me!"

"We are sorry, Tía. We will let you know next time," William said.

"Next time? I said. "There won't be a next time. Trust me."

Alfredito and William kept giggling. "Hey, you two. Stop that. Milagros is right. We should have told her. I don't like these fast rides very much, either. I'm too old for them. Apologize to your aunt."

They did and hugged me. Then, I excused myself and rushed to the bathroom.

From that point forward, I didn't go on any other ride unless Alfredo assured me it was slow. I couldn't trust my nephews.

For the rest of that day, we walked around the park and watched the thousands of people from all over the world who had gathered in this magical place. I could hear some speaking in languages that didn't sound like English or Spanish. I could see why Alfredo had brought me to this place.

Other than my fearful time at Space Mountain, I had a wonderful day watching the shows, enjoying tasty ice cream and food, and discovering each of the park's attractions.

We stayed at one of the Disney resorts for two nights and went to Epcot Center and MGM Studios, two more charming entertainment parks that made me forget I was in my sixties.

While on the drive home, William, who was sitting in the front passenger seat next to his brother, said, "Tía, do you want to see your picture from Space Mountain?"

"Picture? What picture?" I asked.

"I bought it when you went to the bathroom right after we finished that ride."

Walt Disney World

He searched into a plastic bag and handed me a picture. I examined it. In it, William was laughing, but my face looked disfigured with horror. I shook my head. "You are an awful nephew," I said.

"Let me see it," Alfredo, who sat between the window and me, said. I handed it to him, and he examined it. He tried to hold his laughter at first, but after a while, he could no longer do it.

"You are going to laugh at me too?" I asked.

"Come on. It is funny," Alfredo said.

I pressed my lips together. "Well, if I were to analyze it coldly, I guess you're right. I look horrendous but funny. I never knew my face could change that much."

We all laughed, but Las Vegas was next on the agenda, and deep down, I was glad only Alfredo and I were going there.

Being at Walt Disney World allowed me to confront one of my fears. I didn't like the lack of control I felt. But then I thought, was there any aspect of my life in Cuba that I controlled?

Chapter 45

The Next Five Years

Alfredo had planned so many outings during my first trip to the United States that I hardly had time to rest. While in Las Vegas, we stayed at the Treasure Island Hotel and Casino, right off Las Vegas Boulevard—a modestly priced hotel with quick access to the Strip.

Alfredo and I took a walking tour of every hotel in that area, including The Venetian, the most impressive one I had ever seen, with gondolas cruising on a massive pool that resembled the Grand Canal in Venice. We had never visited Venice, but I heard a Spanish couple say this when we were observing the people who were riding the gondolas. We didn't want to spend more money, so we just watched those lucky enough to afford these rides from above.

The Bellagio Hotel, with its beautiful fountains, was as luxurious as The Venetian, but we also enjoyed the less impressive Paris Hotel, with its replica of the Eiffel Tower.

My first trip to the United States surpassed all my expectations—and I gained fourteen pounds in the process! My family asked me to stay. I could have, but something kept pulling me back to Cuba. Was it loyalty to the place where I was born? Was it that my parents and grandmother were buried there? Was there another reason? My brother Alfredo was right. I was an irremediable dreamer.

On the day I left, the whole family came to say goodbye, afraid I would not be able to return. Before I departed toward my assigned gate, Alfredo embraced me tightly. I noticed he was on the verge of tears, and I had never seen him that emotional. What was happening to him? It was probably his age. I heard that men, too, go through hormonal changes.

So I went back to my routine, my piano playing, the long lines to buy the monthly quota, the black-market transactions, and the occasional outing with friends. I no longer had a boyfriend, but I enjoyed going to the movies or the beach with my girlfriends.

A couple of months after my return to Cuba, I received the surprise of my life. My family had applied for my five-year visa. I thought they were crazy, that it would never get approved. Boy, was I wrong! I was so happy. From now on, I would have the best of both worlds. I would travel to the United States as many times as we could afford it. So, for the next five years, every July and December, I visited Alfredo and the family. I loved to spend Christmas with family and watch the excitement when everyone opened their presents while sitting around the lit-up Christmas tree.

I also enjoyed the trip Alfredo and I made to Key West. We saw the Harry S. Truman Little White House, built in 1890, the place where President Truman spent his winter vacations. We drove by La Concha Hotel & Spa, a historical hotel on

Duval Street. I learned that Cuban exiles had left their mark there in 1871 when they founded the San Carlos Institute. It was in this place where José Martí united the exile community to prepare the final phase of his campaign for Cuba's independence from Spain.

While we strolled through the Old Town, we went into one of the piano bars, and Alfredo told the owner that I was a talented pianist from Cuba who was visiting Key West for a brief period. I was so embarrassed. I thought the owner would just tell us to go away, but instead, he asked whether I wanted to sit at the piano and play Cuban tunes for his customers. My eyes lit up.

"Really?" I asked.

"Yes. You can play as much as you want."

I could not believe it. I never imagined playing the piano for vacationgoers in the United States. I walked toward the grand piano and started to play. To my surprise, people kept coming to the piano and leaving their tips in a tall glass that the owner had left on top of it. I must have played for about thirty or forty minutes and made about $50 in tips. Alfredo was so impressed.

"If you are ever in these parts again, feel free to stop by and play," the owner said. "It has been a real treat to meet you."

Alfredo looked at me with so much pride when we left the bar.

"Now, let's have a nice dinner," he said.

"You want to blow the money on a dinner?"

"We live once. Let's make it a memorable one."

The Next Five Years

We could not afford an expensive place, but we found reasonable prices at B.O.'s Fish Wagon on Caroline Street. It wasn't a fancy place, but people told us they had fresh food at competitive prices and a lively atmosphere. So, we shared shrimp, beans and rice, grouper, and onion rings.

Those five years when I could travel back and forth between Cuba and the United States went by so fast. Alfredo took me on three cruises over this period.

Every time I traveled to the United States, my brother had a piece of paradise ready just for me, and I would gain ten to fifteen pounds. My doctor told me not to worry and to eat whatever I wanted because, according to her, "From the moment you land at Jose Marti Airport, you will start to lose weight again without lifting a finger. Cuba has that effect on people, you know."

My doctor had a great sense of humor, and she wasn't wrong. Within a couple of months, I always managed to lose all the weight.

By 2018, my visa expired. Alfredo was already in his mid-seventies, so my nephews did everything they could to renew it. However, their efforts didn't yield any fruit.

On September 22, 2018, a day I will never forget, William called me.

"Tía, are you sitting down?" he said. He sounded calm like he usually did.

"What's going on?"

"I have news for you. Please drink water first."

"William, you're scaring me. Stop playing games and tell me what's going on."

I heard nothing, followed by heavy breaths and his broken voice full of emotion, "Tía, we lost him this afternoon."

I could feel my heart beating faster.

"Lost who?" I asked, suspecting the worst.

"My Dad, Tía. He just faded away."

My emotions flooded my eyes.

"What do you mean? Please don't do this to me! You should not play this way. My brother can't be dead. He was doing fine when I left! Please tell me it isn't true. Not him, too!"

"I'm so sorry, Tía. Just know that he didn't suffer. He died peacefully surrounded by his family," William said through his tears. "He is still here with us and his nurse. We are home. Someone will come pick him up soon."

I started weeping uncontrollably. I had never hurt so much, not even when I lost each of my parents.

"But how? What happened? He wasn't sick!" I shouted.

"Tía, he *was* sick. He just didn't want to tell you."

"What do you mean he was sick?"

"He wasn't producing red blood cells and kept needing blood transfusions. Eventually, the doctors could not keep giving them to him. He wanted to see you happy. He didn't want you to pity him."

"Oh my God! Is that why he organized all those trips? Because he knew they would be the last trips he could take with me? How dare he? How dare he not tell me? Oh my God, William. My brother is gone. I don't know if I can live through

214

this. I will die, Willliam. Life has no meaning without my brother. I don't know that I can go on!"

William and I wept in silence for a while,
mourning for the best father, brother, and human
being we had ever met.

Chapter 46

The Show Must Go On

For several months following the death of my brother, I lost the willingness to go on. I had tried to be positive all my life, to have a glass-half-full view of existence, but life kept taking me apart piece by piece. It took from me everyone I loved.

And then, I became an empty shell.

Nothing mattered. My piano only brought me sadness as I kept playing the songs I played when my brother took me to that piano bar in Key West. I played the same set in my apartment repeatedly, even if it tore me apart to do so. However, feeling the pain of such a magnificent loss was better than feeling nothing at all.

My neighbor Lola sprang into action. I told you about her at the beginning of this story – the one asking me to slow down when I was running downstairs to get my steaks. She became genuinely concerned when one neighbor told another and then another that I wasn't leaving my apartment and that something was very wrong with me. I had even missed my quota for the month. I just didn't want to see anyone.

I didn't know that during Alfredo's visit to Cuba; he gave Lola the telephone numbers of William and Alfredito in case there was ever an emergency. Without telling me anything, Lola called Alfredito and told him what was happening. So he booked a flight to Cuba to see me.

Alfredito also booked a room at the *Hotel Nacional*, the place where my father had been a chef for most of his life. Despite my reluctance, he took me to lunch there. I had not been to that hotel for years, even less for lunch. And yet, there I was, at the luxurious restaurant where my father served for so many years. I could imagine him dressed in his impeccable chef attire, working in the kitchen, making delicious recipes only for me. As I sat there, I wondered if his essence remained here, in the place that gave him his identity.

My father could have left Cuba when his bosses asked him to come with them. So, he was as much of a dreamer as I had been. When I came to this realization while sitting at that restaurant, I also concluded that maybe, just maybe, I could become that dreamer again.

My friend Lola, one of my devoted friends, did much more than call Alfredito. She contacted my friend Alegría, the singer. Her name, as I explained at the beginning of the story, means "happiness." She came to see me and asked me to join a band she was putting together.

In 2019, I joined the band Alegría. I had been a friend of the singer for years, so knowing that I was a composer, she asked me to direct the group. I thought she had lost her mind. Who would hire a group led by women in their sixties? She said, "When life kicks you hard, you kick back!"

We began to play at various venues in Habana, not knowing where our music would take us. I was happy to be playing with a band again, like at the start of my career, getting energy from other band members. I loved it! Occasionally, I would also play the piano at restaurants and bars as a soloist.

It's true what people in Cuba say. He who has friends has a factory. That factory had reconstructed me, and I was back.

Chapter 47

Acapulco

"Where are you going this early in the morning?" my neighbor Lola asked.

"I'm going to stand in line at La Bodega. I had a dream that they would have chicken available today."

I am wearing my best-walking tennis shoes, a pair my brother bought me in 2017, about six years ago, when I was visiting the United States. I am also wearing blue slacks and a white cotton blouse.

"You're crazy. You are going to stand there for nothing."

She's right. I have not been able to find chicken or any meat anywhere.

I heard that the *mipynes* near the area of the Port of Mariel sell them by the box. *Mipynes*. That's a term that surfaced in the past couple of years. They are "private" stores that sell merchandise at exorbitant prices only a few people can afford. And if you think these stores are private, come to my apartment, and I will sell you my entire building for $10,000 cash. There I go again with my silly sense of humor. Of course, they are not private. No one knows who owns them, but everyone knows the government is behind them.

There are also several well-stocked stores in the Vedado neighborhood as well. They have Nutella, Hershey's cocoa powder, and other luxuries I could only imagine. I imagine those are for tourists and high-ranking officials.

The government reported that allowing businesses in Cuba would improve the economic crisis. Still, many people believe that nothing will change if the government remains in control of those businesses. But enough about things I can't control.

Thanks to my friend Lola, my life didn't end when my brother died. Instead, my relationship with my nephews strengthened because, through Alfredito's and his son's visits to Cuba, I realized that little parts of Alfredo still lived in his children and grandchild. I also learned that part of my father never left his beloved hotel. His essence was still present in the dining room where Alfredito and I ate and in the kitchen where those who replaced my father worked. When I was sitting at that restaurant, I remembered how much my father believed in my passion for music. So, I didn't want to waste a minute of the gift he bestowed upon me. I would live my life to the fullest to make him, my mother, and my brother Alfredo proud of me.

In the years that followed Alfredo's passing, my friend Alegría and I defied the concept of age. We learned that age is nothing but a number. If we were lucky enough to have good health, it was our obligation to make the best of our gift. So, we created an extremely popular band, one that was called to radio and television appearances and performed at clubs and restaurants around Havana.

Visitors from other countries took notice. We were so happy when, one rainy evening in 2023, a man with a heavy accent gave us his business card and invited us to perform in Cannes, France. This is the city that is home to the well-known Cannes Film Festival. We immediately accepted, but of course, he would have to make arrangements through the Ministry of Culture. We would later learn that this man was part of France's Communist Party. The Ministry of Culture connected him with the Communist Party in Cuba, and between them, they arranged all the details. We received no compensation, but all expenses were paid.

Imagine how happy we were when we arrived in this city in the French Riviera, the most picturesque place in France. I had never seen so many boats anchored in one place. In Port Pierre Canto, the marina boasted six hundred berths with accommodation for yachts of up to seventy meters. Port of Cannes' marina, in the Old Town, had 650 berths and accommodated yachts of up to sixty-five meters. The city also had even larger docks for smaller boats. You might wonder how I learned all this. I looked it up on the phone I bought with my tips. It's amazing how much one can learn on the internet!

Beautiful Cannes, off the Mediterranean Sea, is a place I could not have imagined even in my dreams: blue marinas dotted by rows of white boats, majestic palm trees lining busy boulevards, beautiful people wearing the latest fashions, strolling Cannes' clean and busy streets.

Acapulco

In October 2023, after spending five days in Cannes, our band, Alegría, had to travel to Cancun, Mexico, for another engagement pre-arranged through the Ministry of Culture in Cuba as part of a cultural exchange with Mexico. We stayed there for three days, performing at a restaurant. Then, we traveled to Acapulco, our last destination, before returning to Cuba.

All the members of our six-person band felt as if we were on top of the world.

After our band completed our first night of performances at a club in Acapulco, an elegantly dressed middle-aged man approached us and said, "I see that you are from Cuba. You are all excellent. Great singing and dancing and superb instrumentality. How long will you be here?"

I explained that we had a three-day commitment.

"I would like to hire you to perform at my restaurant and bar near Acapulco, by the beach. Of course, I would pay for all your expenses and compensate you for your performance. Does that sound like something that would interest you?"

We didn't want to appear overly enthusiastic, so we agreed to meet with him another day to discuss the engagement, which was to start on October 28th.

After returning to our hotel that evening, I pulled a small photo album from my luggage and began to look through it. The pictures in it had a special meaning to me.

"I always see you looking at that album after each performance. Can I see it?" Alegría asked.

I was a little hesitant to give it to her, but I knew she would convince me to do so anyway.

Alegría looked through the pictures and focused on one.

"You look so young in this one!" she said. "And who is the gentleman next to you?"

I shrugged. "Just someone I met many years ago when I was in my early twenties."

Alegría opened her eyes wide. "Oh my God! And you kept his picture for fifty years? This must not be just any guy. What's his name? Were you dating him?"

"His name is Adam. It's a long story."

"Oh no. You're not going to leave me hanging. I know it's late, but we can sleep late tomorrow. Give me every juicy detail."

I shook my head and remained silent for a moment. But she persisted, so I had no other option but to tell her what happened. She listened attentively, evidencing her shock through her expression. She must have thought I was pathetic.

"What a romantic story!" she said. "You didn't keep his address?"

"What was the point if I could not leave Cuba?"

She sighed.

"So, *he* was the one. You stayed in Cuba because, in the back of your mind, you thought and hoped he would return."

"That's insane," I said.

"You can't lie to me. I see how your body shivers when you talk about him. He was the love of your life. Wasn't he?"

I didn't reply.

"I take your silence as a big yes. And you never saw him again?"

I shook my head. "But enough questions for one night. I'm exhausted. It's time for bed."

***

"Life is what happens to you while you're busy making other plans." That's what the extraordinary John Lennon said in his magnificent song *Beautiful Boy*.

We were excited about the October 28th performance. However, on October 25th, in the early hours of the morning, Hurricane Otis, the strongest system ever to hit Acapulco, arrived. The category five hurricane strengthened quickly. A weather station near Acapulco measured a 205-mph wind gust, the highest ever recorded in the world. AP News reported that Acapulco's Diamond Zone, an oceanfront area full of restaurants and hotels, appeared to be mostly underwater. Otis ripped walls and roofs from tall buildings, caused flash floods, and knocked down power. Alegría and I hid in our dark hotel bathroom with our telephones and my photo album while we heard the roar and loud banging outside. It seemed as if the world around was being ripped apart. We were shaking, thinking that our lives would end that night. Minutes turned into hours. I don't remember if we said anything to each other, but we screamed and cried a lot.

When the winds finally died down, we carefully left the bathroom. Our room was destroyed. Even the bed was gone! We had lost the luggage, the sheet music, and the instruments. Although we had our telephones, there was no internet.

When we walked outside, the once idyllic tourist area looked like a war zone. The main roads were inaccessible and choked with mud. Massive looting exacerbated an already chaotic situation, and our fight for survival ensued. We walked for miles looking for water. We finally found water and snacks in a store that the hurricane had destroyed. We took what we could.

"I can't believe this," I said as I walked outside the store with the heavy gallons. "I never thought that my life could be worse than it is for ordinary Cubans living on the island."

You never genuinely appreciate how precious life is until you look at death in the face. Hurricane Otis showed me how much fight I still had within me. Life was testing me again, and this was not a test I was willing to lose.

***

Now, we have come full circle, and I am back to where this story began. We reconnected with our band members a few hours after Otis passed. Some of them were much younger than us, so it was easier for them to search for food and water.

The van from the embassy is almost here. In a couple of days, we will be back in Cuba. I miss my thin mattress and my unpainted apartment.

I miss waiting for a man who might never come.

Epilogue

I am sitting in front of a white grand piano in a luxurious room full of light, as big as a baseball stadium. The room is packed with the happiest people I have ever seen. But something has changed. I am no longer playing for tips but for myself.

I feel as joyful as I did when Alfredo took me to the piano bar in Key West. My eyes close as I play and picture him. It makes me so happy to see him in my mind. I open my eyes, and he is standing by my piano with a glowing smile.

"Alfredo! I missed you so much," I say.

"I missed you too," he replies.

"But don't think I will ever forgive you for leaving me the way you did. That was unforgivable!"

"You know I had to. I couldn't put you through all the pain."

"You didn't have to protect me. I wanted to be there for you. I'm your sister, for God's sake."

"It was better that way," he says. "Remember when you were a child? Mom used to say that if you removed the bandaid quickly, it would hurt less than if you did it slowly. That's all I did."

"You had no right to do that to me. I wanted to be there and hold your hand. That's what siblings do."

226

Epilogue

"I didn't want to see my little sister sad. Maybe I was protecting myself, too, from the pain of seeing you suffer. Would you forgive me?"

"I'll think about it," I say.

"I see that your playing has only gotten better through the years."

"It feels good to play for myself for a change without a care in the world."

He smiles and watches me play. As I play, I look around the room, and in the distance, I see my parents dancing together to my music. They look so joyful. And are those Laura and Rio standing a few feet away from my parents? They look in my direction and wave at me. I stop playing for a moment and wave back. I was about to get up to go toward them, but I hear a voice.

"Beautiful lady," a man says in perfect Spanish. "Would you be so kind as to play my favorite song, *Bésame Mucho*?"

I stare at him while I start to play the song he requested. There is something familiar about his face. Then I stop playing and wave my finger at him.

"I know you," I say.

He smiles.

"A lot of time has passed. A lifetime, in fact," he replies.

"You look so different."

"It's understandable. I don't look like the man you once knew. To me, however, you look the same. I am happy that at least you recognized me."

"How could I not?" I say. "I have been glancing at a picture of those eyes for over sixty years."

227

Epilogue

He flashes a youthful smile and reaches for my hand.

Pictures

My fifteenth birthday. Laura and Rio are on the left of the picture. My brother Alfredo, his wife, and Alfredito are on the right. My mother is behind me, next to Laura. Year – 1966

My grandmother Reimunda with Laura and Berta on either side.

My parents and Alfredo

Pictures

Alfredo and his bride on his wedding day.

My piano and I at the house in Mantilla. On top of the piano is a picture of Laura and Rio on their wedding day.

Acknowledgments

Lázara Portomeñe, for the testimonies about her life that formed the basis for this book.

William Portomeñe (owner of Portomene LaSuite Hair Salon in Miami) for his recommendations.

Conchita Hernandez Hicks (author of *Leaving Havana*) and Marta Mayer, for being fantastic beta readers and providing valuable recommendations.

Susana Mueller, from Susanabooks, for designing a superb book cover and being a beta reader for this manuscript. A friend told me that the cover looks like a masterpiece. I agree. Thank you, Susana, for your vision.

Mary McCullough, for allowing me to use the beautiful picture of Budapest.

The Facebook group *All Things Cuban*, thank you for providing an essential forum for disseminating Cuban history and culture.

The Facebook group *Women Reading Great Books, thank you* for providing an essential outlet for authors and readers.

Acknowledgments

My husband, Ivan, for making suggestions about various chapters of this book. His contributions have been invaluable.

My son Ivan and his wife, for providing recommendations about the book's cover.

My mother-in-law, Madeline, and my sister, Lissette, for their contributions.

My mother, Milagros, for being the intellectual author of my life and still guiding my steps, even after her death.

To all the readers who continue to support me and share my posts, and to all the book clubs that have selected my books—there are too many to mention.

About the Author

Betty Viamontes was born in Havana, Cuba. At age fifteen, Betty and her family crossed the Florida Straits in an overcrowded shrimp boat on a stormy night when many families perished. After almost twelve years of separation, this trip would reunite the family with Betty's father in the United States. Betty Viamontes completed graduate studies at the University of South Florida. She began to dedicate her life to capturing the stories of people without a voice. Her stories have traveled the world, from the award-winning *Waiting on Zapote Street* to the No. 1 new release, *The Girl from White Creek*.

Other works include:

Havana: A Son's Journey Home

The Dance of the Rose

Candela's Secrets and Other Havana Stories

Flight of the Tocororo (Collaboration)

Brothers: A Pedro Pan Stories (Awarded Best Fiction 2022)

Seeking Closure: The Pedro Pan Girls

Love Letters from Cuba

About the Author

Crossing North: Tribulations of a Cuban Doctor

Orchids in the Shadows

Raining Over Teresa: From Mother to Hero

Flight of the Tocororo (collaboration with Susana Mueller)

The above books are available in English and Spanish. *Waiting on Zapote Street* was one of the winners of The Latino Books Into Movies award and has been selected by a United Nations women's book club and many others.

Her works have appeared in various publications, including the prestigious literary journal *The Mailer Review*.

Made in the USA
Columbia, SC
27 September 2025

70318906R00134